COMMERCIAL REAL ESTATE 101

TRUMP
UNIVERSITY

COMMERCIAL REAL ESTATE 101

How Small Investors Can Get Started and Make It Big

DAVID LINDAHL

WILEY

John Wiley & Sons, Inc.

Published by John Wiley & Sons, Inc., Hoboken, New Jersey
Published simultaneously in Canada

For general information on our other products and services or for technical support, please contact our Customer Care Department within the United States at (800) 762-2974, outside the United States at (317) 572-3993 or fax (317) 572-4002.

Wiley also publishes its books in a variety of electronic formats. Some content that appears in print may not be available in electronic books. For more information about Wiley products, visit our web site at www.wiley.com.

Library of Congress Cataloging-in-Publication Data

Lindhal, David.
 Trump University commercial real estate 101: how small investors can get started and make it big/David Lindahl.
  p. cm
 Includes index.
 ISBN 978-0-470-38035-2 (cloth)
  1. Commercial real estate. 2. Real estate investment. 3. Commercial real estate—United States. 4. Real estate investment—United States. I. Title.
 HD1393.55.L56 2008
 332.63'24—dc22
                                                                        2008032211

Printed in the United States of America.

10 9 8 7 6 5 4 3 2

CONTENTS

CONTENTS

CONTENTS

CONTENTS

FOREWORD TO TRUMP UNIVERSITY COMMERCIAL REAL ESTATE 101

The only way to run an organization as large as mine is to be highly efficient. The competition is simply too great to trust mere theory. Therefore I use tested and proven methods whenever possible.

I built Trump University on the same principle. If you're looking for nice-sounding theory, you won't find it in my organization. I've made sure that the curriculum is built on a rock-solid foundation of proven methods for building your business.

The book you are holding, Trump University Commercial Real Estate 101, is no different. I chose David Lindahl to write it because he's not only a highly successful investor, but he has a knack for clarity in explaining commercial real estate investing.

Clarity is especially important when it comes to this topic. Unlike investing in single-family homes, it's possible to be overwhelmed by the size and purchase price of commercial properties. Don't let that deter you from pursuing your dreams! Trust me: You don't have to implement everything right away. Just take one investing step at a time. The real key to success is to get moving and take those steps.

You've made a smart move by getting your commercial real estate investing advice from Trump University. Study this book and follow the advice. Who knows—someday you and I may own properties next to each other.

DONALD J. TRUMP

1

COMMERCIAL REAL ESTATE INVESTING

IT'S NOT ONLY FOR BILLIONAIRES

Do you have the mind-set of a winner?

Here's how a billionaire-wannabe thinks: "Someday, if I'm as wealthy as Donald Trump, I'd love to own a bunch of properties in my town."

Here's how a future billionaire thinks: "The way to become as wealthy as Donald Trump is to start owning commercial property in my town."

Commercial property isn't your destination; it's the way you will reach it.

COMMERCIAL REAL ESTATE IS THE INVISIBLE GIANT

You can't pick up a newspaper these days without seeing some story—usually negative—about the residential real estate market. But there's another, quiet, vast real estate market that is quite independent of the ups and downs of residential property.

Just what is commercial real estate? It's

- Office buildings (all the way from skyscrapers down to a small building with a dental office in it)
- Apartment buildings with five or more units
- Stores, whether they're in big malls or small, local shopping centers
- Hotels and restaurants
- Industrial space (factories, warehouses, and so on)

It's no wonder that the value of U.S. commercial real estate is many trillions of dollars, given that we spend most of our waking hours working in it, shopping in it, and even celebrating and vacationing in it.

I'm not going to keep you in suspense. Here's a huge secret, right on the first pages of this book:

> The wealth opportunity with commercial real estate is enormous for the very reason that most people think they could never own it.

If investors only understood how it's possible to make a fortune from commercial real estate, they would ruin the market for the rest of us. So thank your lucky stars that commercial real estate remains shrouded in myth and misinformation for millions of real estate investors.

They convince themselves that it's not worth doing commercial real estate because they imagine a series of huge barriers in their way. Here are just three of the many psychological barriers to entry:

- "The bigger the building, the bigger the down payment that I need."
- "I couldn't possibly own a shopping center; I know nothing about retail sales."
- "All the good deals must have long since been picked over: I'll see only the lousy ones."

I recognize that even you might be spooked by some of these psychological barriers. That's okay: We cover each of them in this book. By the time you're finished reading, you'll have a clear plan for how to go from where you are right now to owning that first commercial property.

Right away, I can tell that *you* are different. After all, you're not frozen in your tracks, unwilling to consider commercial real estate. In fact, you've taken the crucial step of buying and actually reading this book. You may find this hard to believe, but you've just put yourself ahead of 80 percent of those billionaire-wannabes.

There are wonderful, perceived *force fields* around commercial real estate that keep most investors out. Let's look at some of the excellent benefits you'll enjoy once you're part of this informal but highly successful club.

Six Reasons to Invest in Commercial Real Estate

It's Not about Your Wealth or Lack of It—It's about the Property

I got started in real estate with less than $800 to my name. I now own a very large portfolio of commercial real estate. It's not as big as Donald Trump's, but I'm getting there!

You may be in a situation that is similar to mine at the beginning: no money, no knowledge of real estate, no connections, and working a full-time job.

What was my big break? I recognized two life-changing principles early on, and I'm now handing them to you:

Principle #1: The better the deal, the less people focus on me and the more they focus on getting that deal. If I had a clear winner on my hands, they really could not care less that I was an inexperienced investor. They just wanted the deal.

Principle #2: Real estate is an inefficient market. That means bad, good, and great deals are being generated all the time, and they pop up in unexpected places.

If you want to buy stock in Starbucks, you'll get the same price whether you're in Peoria or Pakistan. But there is no such central clearinghouse for real estate deals. On any given day, hundreds of business situations change in your town: Companies merge, expand, and decide to relocate. Contracts are awarded, marketing campaigns take off, and products get publicity. Other companies change hands because the owner dies or retires. These events often result in a property being put up for sale. There is no single way that happens. Instead, the property may be listed by a broker, or an ad may appear in the paper. The owner may be thinking about whether to sell when he meets someone at a party and they strike up a conversation.

Sometimes the owner is out of state or even out of the country and does not know any local buyers or brokers. Unlike that Starbucks stock, this hodge-podge of a real estate market makes for great opportunities that were hidden yesterday, and lie uncovered today.

After you read and follow my system for attracting deals, two things will happen: You'll see a lot of worthless deals; and every so often you'll come across a real gem.

That's why you can start from where you are right now, and make a fortune in commercial real estate. Your marketing systems will eventually find a gem that's so good, no one will care that it's your first deal.

Commercial Real Estate Will Open Up a Huge Segment of Your Local Market That You Previously Avoided

Confining yourself to investing only in single-family homes is like looking at your town through a drinking straw. The whole town is there, but your view is incredibly narrow.

Once you are comfortable with my systems for investing in commercial property, you'll be throwing that straw away. Everywhere you look, you will see opportunities that never occurred to you before. You will have become a *transaction engineer*.

- Maybe there is a parcel of land next to a highway where you can now envision a small office building or strip mall. You could buy the land and flip it to a developer for a nice profit.
- Maybe there is a run-down *strip mall* (several stores next to each other in a row) that you pass every day while driving to work. You notice that with some simple improvements this area could be getting much more business.
- You see a *For Sale* sign on a small office building, and contact the owner. You realize that the numbers work for you to buy and hold that property for long-term cash flow and appreciation.

Let your competitors wrestle each other over the single-family home market. Commercial real estate will vastly broaden your horizons.

Don't get me wrong: I'm not suggesting that you must become expert at every type of property. I just want to open your eyes to the possibilities—right in your own backyard—that you may not have ever considered.

You have to start somewhere, so it's fine to pick one type of property and get good at it. But don't stop there. The more property types you can invest in, the easier it will be to find a great opportunity.

Start anywhere you like—but make sure that you *start*. You *do* want to be a transaction engineer, but you do not want to have analysis paralysis, where you never quite get around to making offers and doing deals.

Later we'll talk about how to take the weight off your shoulders and how to build a low-cost team of professionals to do the heavy lifting.

Less Competition: They're Scared Off Because They Don't Know the Secrets You'll Discover in This Book

In my investing and speaking travels around the United States, I talk with a great many people. One of the most common excuses I hear for not getting involved in real estate is: "I'd love to, Dave, but you don't understand how severe the competition is in my area."

I have two responses to that: First, if you have the right marketing systems in place, you'll be successful regardless of how much competition there is. Second, that's all the more reason to branch out from single-family homes into commercial property, where there are fewer investors.

Notice that I said *branch out* and not *do instead*. I still invest in single-family houses when a great deal comes along. It's like finding money on the street, only this kind of money is 10 or 20 thousand bucks!

There's no need to *stop* investing in one type of property, once you know how to invest that way. Instead, you simply focus on one type while keeping your eyes open to all the other possibilities that come your way.

Later in this book, we'll systematically explore each of the myths surrounding commercial properties, and how you can confidently move forward where other people fear to tread.

Cash Flow

Cash flow is king. It will set you free.

Early in my investing career, I thought I had it made. I had gone from being a dirt-poor landscaper (ha-ha) to a multimillionaire in just under four years. There was only one small problem:

I couldn't pay my bills.

How could that be? It was because my millions were on paper. I truly did have that wealth, but it was tied to the eventual sale or refinancing of my properties. I was not receiving a regular monthly check.

That's when the next part of my education occurred. I realized that the true lubricant of business was steady cash flow. It didn't matter how powerful my real estate engine was; without that cash flow, the gears would grind to a halt.

Commercial property provides this business lubricant—cash flow—in superior amounts. Certainly, you can become wealthy by investing in single-family homes. But you better be doing a string of them in quick succession in order to provide the cash flow you need from month to month. That sounds like a lot of work to me.

With even a single commercial property, you can look forward to a nice check being dropped into your mailbox every month like clockwork.

At first the checks may be smaller, because your number-one priority is to cover the cash flow needs of the property. You'll have operating expenses that must be paid each month, and *capital expenses* (major repairs) that will come up from time to time.

If you use a tested-and-proven system to buy right, you'll have a cushion of cash flow that more than covers the property needs. You get to pocket the rest of that money.

Your first goal may be to accumulate enough positive cash flow so that it equals what you are earning in your full-time job. Then you'll have the option to quit that job and become a full-time investor.

After that goal is fulfilled, no doubt you'll have other ones: Perhaps you'll use the additional cash flow to purchase more properties. Maybe you'll use it to help a struggling loved one, send your kids to college, go on a long vacation, or all of the above.

Cash flow will indeed set you free. It will give you the confidence and the ability to do the things in life that you couldn't do before.

You Can Think Big But Still Start Very Small

You've heard Donald Trump say it: "If you're going to think, you might as well think big."

Commercial property has two very important characteristics: It allows you to get as big as your imagination will let you, but it also allows you to start as small as you like.

Dreams without action are not impressive. Commercial property is the path from your dreams and modest initial actions all the way up to your ultimate financial goals.

I remember sitting at a restaurant in Boston with a friend, James Romeo. At the time I owned several small multi-family buildings. He knew that I had been spending a lot of time in my investment business and that I had accumulated a nice little portfolio.

James asked if I would be available to go to a social event he had planned. I told him I had to look at some new properties. He sighed and said, "Dave, when will enough be enough?" I looked out the window and said, "When I buy *that*." I was pointing at the Prudential Tower skyscraper.

He rolled his eyes, because he knew the biggest thing I owned was a six-family building. But I was already thinking big back then. I later made sure to send James a magazine that featured my story and described my portfolio, which did not include the Prudential Tower, but had increased 20 times since we met for lunch that day.

Start as small as you like, but again the most important thing is to *start*. Once you see the system working for you and that monthly cash flow check being delivered, you'll soon be thinking ever bigger. You will realize that economies of scale favor larger properties and it's actually *easier* to own larger properties, because they can support a larger team to run them for you.

When You Follow Proven Systems, Commercial Properties Offer Lower Risk

I know: How can something bigger than a house have less risk than a house? It seems odd, but it's true.

Let's say you're renting out a single-family residence. If you lose your tenant, you've lost 100 percent of your income. If you can't find another tenant, pronto, you'll be covering the next mortgage payment from your own pocket.

In a commercial property, you'll have several tenants, and even hundreds. You still may lose one, but the others will continue to pay rent. This cash flow should cover most, if not all, of your mortgage payment. Each tenant is like a pillar supporting your investment. If you ask me, it's better to have lots of pillars, rather than just one.

How You Can Make Money from Commercial Investing

With some investments you simply try to buy low and sell high. Commercial real estate gives you a whole rainbow of opportunities to profit. Let's briefly look at some of them.

Equity Build-Up

This is where the real money is. Equity build-up happens in two ways.

The first is through paying down the mortgage principal. You'll have your tenants to thank for that, whether it's a multi-family, office, retail space, or another type of property.

Each month they will give you a big slice of their income in the form of rent checks. You use a portion of that money to make the mortgage payment. In one sense, your tenants go to work each morning to buy the building *for* you. What a country!

I remember when I first heard of this concept. I was watching a television documentary on the life of Harry Helmsley. When asked why he began investing in commercial properties, Harry said, "I always liked the idea that a group of people would pool their money together to pay off the mortgage on my building. I also liked the idea that they would give me extra money at the end of the month that I could use to reinvest, put into a savings account, or just have some fun with."

That was enough inspiration for me!

The second way to get equity build-up is through appreciation. Over time, real estate values in most areas go up. Yes, appreciation is subject to cycles, but over the long term, the line on the graph trends upward. Some markets appreciate faster than others. The markets on the East and West coasts tend to appreciate higher and faster than markets in the Midwest.

Cash flow may be the vital lubricant of your real estate machine, but appreciation is the giant engine. Cash flow allows you to run your properties, quit your job, and start enjoying the finer things in life. Appreciation comes more slowly, but has the potential to add many zeros to your bank account.

Emerging Markets

Real estate investing is my focus, but the study of emerging markets is my passion. At any given time—regardless of what the national economy is doing—there are markets around the United States that are just on the verge of explosive growth.

They are about to appreciate much faster than other markets around the country, and they can make you a great deal of money in a short period. My book, *Emerging Real Estate Markets*, describes in much more detail how to find and profit from these markets.

The key concept to understand is that *all real estate markets are local*. It doesn't matter what the national headlines are screaming. A factory shuts down in one town, and somewhere else an oil company has just opened a new branch office. A Michigan automaker announces more layoffs, but a foreign automaker announces plans to build a factory in Kentucky.

There are two tricks to making money in emerging markets: First, you must be able to locate these markets slightly before most other investors know that they are good. Second, you must be willing to invest when other people think you're crazy.

That's because you will be *buying low*, or investing when other people don't see the value. That positions you to *sell high*—in other words, when other people think you're crazy for selling too soon.

Just get used to the feeling of people thinking you're crazy. It's not hard to do, because soon you'll be much wealthier than they are!

There are emerging markets for commercial properties all around the United States at any given time. The best part is, different types of commercial property follow different paths in the market cycle. Simply because a market is emerging for apartments does not mean that it is emerging for retail space.

As a matter of fact, retail space generally lags behind apartments: First come the announcements that new job opportunities will be opening up in an area. That creates a demand for office space.

Then the people who will work in those offices begin to move into town. Because homes can't be built fast enough, the apartment market suddenly heats up.

Many people want to see if their job will work out, and they want to get a good feel for the community. They check things out by renting first. After their leases expire, they start to buy single-family houses. Retail space tends to follow housing surges, as merchants realize they can make money by moving closer to where people live and work.

Discovering how to recognize the signs of emerging markets—and then acting on that knowledge—will make you a very rich person.

Forced Appreciation

This is one of the fastest ways to make money with commercial properties. The concept is also called a *value play*. Whenever you look at a deal, always look for ways to force appreciation beyond what the local market may naturally generate.

To force appreciation, you must find a deal with a slight problem. It won't be a problem for *you*, but it's been a nagging issue for the previous owner. Maybe he's been afraid to raise rents, so his rents are under market. Maybe he is charging the correct amount for rent, but has higher-than-normal vacancies. Perhaps his expenses are running high.

These are all opportunities to buy a property with a built-in reward, as long as you buy based on the *actual numbers*. That is the key to buying right with commercial properties.

Let me take a minute to talk about the numbers that a potential seller will propose to you. Most sellers try to sell based on projected or *pro forma* numbers. This means that they are basing their price on what they *think* you can earn after you buy the property. The problem with *pro forma* numbers is they are not real. You are buying based on future cash flows that may never materialize.

That is a speculator's game, and way too risky for my blood. If you want to gamble, go to Vegas. If you want to make solid investments, base them on actual results.

Back to forced appreciation: All you have to do is raise rents up to market levels. You'll first have to wait until leases expire, because leases transfer with ownership. Apartments usually have one-year leases. Office buildings and other commercial properties have 3-year to 20-year leases.

Here's why raising rents also raises your property value: Commercial properties are primarily valued on multiples of their cash flow. (There are two other valuation methods that I discuss later in the book, but cash flow is the main one.) This means that for each notch that you raise your *net operating income*, you've just raised the value of your property by multiple notches.

One of my favorite value plays is to find a property with higher-than-normal expenses. Most properties operate with expenses of about 50 percent of gross income. When you see the actual financials of a property with higher expenses, determine if you can lower those expenses to the average level. (Later I show you how.) If you can, you may have a winner on your hands. Without doing any significant work to the property, you can improve net operating income and truly improve the property value.

Repositioning

This is a special type of value play, and one of my favorites. When you *reposition* a property, you change the tenant base or significantly alter the appearance of the property. Sometimes you do both.

You may find a property that needs some tender loving care. We call this *deferred maintenance*. Maybe it's an okay property, but it hasn't been upgraded in over a decade. It may look tired and out-of-date. There may also be the wrong type of tenant leasing the space.

Back when I was broke, I would visit a suburban strip mall in Hingham, Massachusetts. Its *anchor tenant* (that is, its biggest store) was a discount department chain. Another store was even *more* discount: It specialized in dinged-up furniture and flawed clothing. The mall included other typical shops, such as a pizza joint and a Laundromat. For years the mall had languished as a working-class shopping center.

In the meantime, the demographics in Hingham had changed. The city could now support higher-end enterprise. The working-class mall gained a new life and was repositioned as the nation's first *lifestyle center*. In place of the blue-collar stores, high-end shops like Williams Sonoma, Whole Foods, and Panera Bread moved into the refurbished spaces. The place took off, and is now one of the most popular shopping centers in the area.

Apartments are sometimes great candidates for repositioning. Let's say that you find a tired apartment building in a good area. This property has not been kept up well, so it's attracting tenants who are even less well-kept.

To reposition the building, you first spruce up the exterior, focusing on the siding, roofing, and parking lot. You upgrade the landscaping, put new signage on the property, and create a nice leasing office. You then work on certain strategic improvements inside the property.

With the property now looking much better, it's time to reposition those tenants. You get rid of the tenants who pay slowly, never pay at all, or are criminally inclined. Replace them with the tenant profile that you are targeting.

This is a process that can take several months, absorbing more time and money than the simple value-play of raising rents. The rewards can be quite spectacular, though. Not only can you fill your vacant units, but soon all of the units are paying substantially more in rent. Because your property value is calculated at a multiple of the net operating income, you've just skyrocketed the worth of the property.

When you come across a property that fits the profile I just described, you should definitely consider it for repositioning. I wrote an entire book on the topic called *Multi-Family Millions*, published by John Wiley & Sons. This concept of making low-cost, high-payoff changes to both a property and its tenants is enormously powerful.

Tax Deferral Through 1031 Exchanges

The Declaration of Independence may tell us that *all men are created equal*, but the government definitely favors us real estate investors!

Not only do we get to depreciate (that is, take a tax deduction on) the value of our investment real estate, but we also get to use an astonishingly powerful tool called a *Section 1031 Tax-Deferred Exchange*.

It's like an IRA account on baseball steroids. You can legally sell one property and buy another, while deferring all tax payments on your profits. That doesn't sound impressive until you stop to think about it.

Let me give you an example. Say you bought an office building for $1 million and you sold it two years later for $1.5 million. To make this very simple, I will assume that there are no closing costs in the transaction. This means that you will walk away with a $500,000 profit.

You can't walk far, though, because your friendly IRS agent is standing there, wanting 15 percent of your profit to cover your long-term capital gains tax. So you hand him $75,000 of your profit, leaving you with $425,000 to reinvest.

If you put 20 percent down on your next property, you could afford to purchase one for $2,125,000, again assuming no closing costs. Not bad.

With the 1031 Tax-Deferred Exchange, however, you can tell the friendly IRS agent that all of your profit is going right into your next property. (There are detailed rules on how to do this, but just bear with me while I describe the general principles.) The IRS man nods, steps aside, and tells you to have a nice day.

Because you can use all of your profits for a down payment on the next deal, you can buy a property worth $2,500,000 ($500,000 is 20 percent down on $2,500,000). You've just bought a property that's $375,000 larger, with that much more potential for cash flow and appreciation.

You can do this as many times as you wish, and each instance will be tax-deferred. Yes, eventually you will pay taxes on that profit. But it's now much greater profit, because 100 percent of your proceeds have been working for you, instead of losing a portion of the profit going to tax payments after each transaction.

The second-best part is that the process is entirely aboveboard. No tax loopholes are involved. And what's the *very* best part? You've made much more money!

Imagine exchanging the same properties over and over again. After not many transactions, you could easily be buying properties worth millions, tens of millions, or even more.

IN THE NEXT CHAPTER

This chapter has been merely an appetizer. I wanted to give you a taste of what an excellent decision you made by picking up this book. Commercial real estate is a gem that we all see every day, and is psychologically off-limits to most investors—but not to you.

It's time to buckle up, because in the next chapter I show you how to find your very first commercial cash cow that you can milk for a good long time.

2

How to Read a Market

When most of us look at a stream, we see water running through a field, or perhaps we appreciate the nice landscape. A seasoned fisherman looks at the same stream in an entirely different way: He *reads* the stream, noticing the currents, eddies, and contours. At a glance, he can focus on the very best places to drop his fishing line and find the big ones.

It's no different with real estate. Most people have a vague sense of how their town is doing. Ask them, and they'll say "Pretty good," or "We're kinda hurting right now," or "I've never seen it this bad." These are generalities.

When a professional *reads* a real estate market, it's altogether a different story. She can tell you specifics about construction, job growth, the *path of progress*, and much more. Even more impressive is her ability to predict the future. Yes, when you understand the concept of *leading indicators* and what to look for in a market, you can quickly get a solid idea of what that market will be like in months and even years into the future.

In order to understand how to read any market, you first must become familiar with the four main phases of the commercial real estate market cycle:

1. Buyers' Market, Phase I
2. Buyers' Market, Phase II
3. Sellers' Market, Phase I
4. Sellers' Market, Phase II

Every type of commercial property follows these four phases, though they may be in different parts of the cycle at any given time. For instance, apartment investments will experience strength before retail does. That's because renters can move into apartments very quickly after, say, a new factory opens in town. Retail establishments will first notice the stronger consumer demand and then build to take advantage of it. It's simply *cause and effect*.

How long does it take for a market to complete a full rotation? It depends on the dynamics of that market. The average market cycle lasts between 10 and 25 years. Cities on the East Coast and West Coast tend to change more quickly from phase to phase than do cities in the heartland of America.

In fact, coastal cities tend to have meteoric rises and stonelike falls. In the long periods of time between sudden rises and abrupt falls, investors tend to experience slow, steady growth, and sometimes stagnation, for quite some time.

Buyers' Market, Phase I

Each phase in the market exhibits unique characteristics that you can identify if you're watching for them. In a Buyers' Market, Phase I, you will find a market that's oversupplied with commercial properties. Supply is one of the key market forces that causes a market to go from boom to bust and back again.

At all downturns of a market, oversupply will be present. Think of a real estate market as if it were the largest aircraft carrier on the ocean. The captain can decide within an instant to change direction, but the ship will take some time to respond to the captain's orders. If he becomes impatient and orders an even greater course change—before the ship has responded to the first order, now he has over-corrected.

This also happens in real estate markets. Investors make snap judgments based on strengths that they see *right now*. They put new construction in motion. Keep in mind that it can take three years or longer for the planning, permitting, and construction phases to be completed. In the meantime, investors at first are delighted to see even more demand in the market. That generates even more construction activity.

Finally that great ship—this load of real estate deals—eventually comes online and the market has overcorrected, just like the ship with the impatient captain. There's now a glut of new properties available, and they're overpriced, too. Why? Because they were built when prices were high. Their costs were therefore higher.

Now the supply suddenly outstrips demand, and price-cutting takes hold. To make matters worse, phase I of a buyers' market also tends to coincide with stagnant or negative job growth in the area.

As the market cools, companies stop expanding and may even begin to lay off workers. Retail receipts drop, office space becomes abundant, and apartments begin to see higher vacancies. These are the characteristics of an oversupplied market.

When the new commercial space comes online, there will be more of it than there are people or businesses to occupy it. Desperate owners forget their rosy profit spreadsheets and slash rental rates to get that space filled and start seeing income—any income.

In addition to the key factor of supply, job growth is a significant market force. In a Buyers' Market, Phase I, there is none. Jobs had started to slow down or leave the area in the previous Sellers' Market, Phase II. At the beginning of a Buyer's Market, Phase I, job losses are still taking place.

The market will reach a point at which unemployment peaks and investment property values will decline to their lowest level of any phase in the cycle.

When Jobs Become the Engine

For a city or town to move to a Buyers' Market, Phase II—the next phase in the cycle—its leaders must do something to increase employment opportunities. When jobs are created, people begin to migrate back into a community, population increases, vacant spaces begin to fill, and at last rents once again begin to climb.

In order to attract job growth, the first necessary element is strong local leadership. If local government is not committed to change—or if its only activity is finger-pointing about who's to blame for the lousy economy—the area will continue to wallow in a Buyers' Market, Phase I.

Each city has a master plan to guide it to the next round of growth. City leadership creates the plan to facilitate growth. To get your own copy of the master plan, call the local economic development committee and speak with a local official. He will be happy to talk with you and tell you about all the wonderful things in the city that are happening, or soon will be. He knows the city needs investors like you in order to spark the next round of growth.

You must be cautious when viewing the master plan, though. First determine when it was last updated. Is it fresh, or is it one of those documents that took time and energy to compile, but no one pays any attention to?

If it was written ten years ago and has not been updated, city leadership is not proactive.

Next, determine whether the city has actually taken action on the plan. A continuously updated plan that never comes to fruition is simply a work of fiction.

In the plan, you should see many areas that are labeled *revitalization zones*. These are usually downtrodden areas filled with obsolete buildings. The city usually creates a plan to spur business growth and development in these areas. They can be great places to invest, but only if the city has spent significant money to make its plan a reality, and is clearly taking action.

Until you see that happen, leave your money in your pocket. Don't get stuck buying into that work of fiction that goes nowhere, and has a sad ending.

BUYERS' MARKET, PHASE II

If the city leadership is on the ball, new jobs will begin to emerge in the city. Following the jobs, people will begin to migrate back to the city. The market slowly absorbs its oversupply of properties. Rental spaces fill up. Not only does occupancy increase, but there is a decline in how long properties and retail and office space stay on the market.

As even more jobs come into the area, the pace quickens. Boarded-up residential and commercial properties come to life as investors rehab them and put them back on the market.

During the previous phase—Buyers' Market, Phase I—bank fore-closures had risen to their highest levels. It's typical in the later stage of a Buyers' Market, Phase II, for competition for these bank foreclosures to become fierce. Both national and local investors now realize that there is money to be made in this market. Word gets around and both experienced and new investors circle this market on their maps.

As the market continues to improve, properties morph from being occupied by anyone who can fog a mirror and pay a few dollars in rent, to fulfilling their *highest and best use*. The quality of businesses and tenants improves because they can afford to pay higher rent.

Rents and lease rates were at their lowest levels in the earlier Buyers' Market, Phase I, but they're now on the move. Because of this, property values also rise. Commercial property values rise fairly quickly, because they are largely valued as a function of their income, which is getting better all the time.

This is the very beginning stage of an *emerging market*. Any investor can see this new activity taking place. Only the savvy investors can look at the earlier Buyers' Market, Phase I, and know that this Phase II market is about to occur. They—and you—know this by doing your research and looking for certain market forces taking place.

Oddly enough, local property owners are the most likely to be blind to all the signs of recovery at first. They're the last to see it because their vision is so clouded by the pain they've been through in the last few years. They watched unemployment increase and saw the glut of properties that choked the market. They felt constant pain as revenues dropped, but their payments to lenders did not.

In the midst of all the swearing they did at the terrible market, they swore they would not invest in the area again. After all, they see no construction happening, and figure that the market is still dead.

These are fabulous sellers for you! They're still hurting and looking for someone to dump their properties on when you come along, *maybe* interested in buying.

They breathe a giant sigh of relief when you slide that check across the closing table. Their long nightmare is over.

The major oversupply is just starting to be absorbed, though, and rent levels have not grown high enough to support the building of new properties.

Because this city had an aggressive program to attract jobs, companies have committed to the area. Those plans transform from commitments to actual, breathing people signing up for those new jobs.

As jobs come in, other jobs are created. For every one professional job that comes into an area, another three to four service jobs are created to support that professional. This is called the *Multiplier Effect*.

If a city expects to increase its labor force by 4,000 new nonagricultural jobs, you can expect a total employment increase of 12,000 to 18,000. This ripple effect will positively affect each type of commercial property, although—as I said before—apartments will see the benefits before retail does.

As jobs come into an area, competition for labor begins to increase, and so do salaries. There is now more disposable income that gets reinvested into the community in the form of restaurant and shopping revenues. The prosperity phase is beginning.

Sellers' Market, Phase I

This is the second half of the emerging market. It occurs when a market reaches *equilibrium*. Rental and lease rates have risen to the level that can support new construction of commercial properties.

In this phase, even the local die-hard pessimists have become believers. Everyone is convinced that the good times are here to stay, and money flows into the market. Investors from far away now read about the market and add to the inflow of money.

With all these investors now seeing positive signs everywhere they look, demand for investment properties is at the highest point of any phase in the cycle.

Demand now increases even more and soon surpasses the supply of investment properties. The same is true of commercial space and rental units. Construction again takes off. Properties sell very quickly and *time on the market* reaches its lowest point of all the phases.

Needless to say, this phase is very competitive for property buyers. Bidding wars occur when properties come onto the market. Buyers offer more than asking price to ensure they buy *something* in this hot market.

Speculation is in full swing. Raw land is snatched up for development, and properties that suffer from any sort of obsolescence are bought and quickly converted to their highest and best use.

Just try getting a contractor to do repairs to your property at this point in the cycle! You won't get your calls returned, because the contractors have decided to become developers: They see the money that's being made.

Employment continues to increase, as do wages. The number of people per household decreases as people start new jobs and move away from the family sanctuaries that housed them during the lean times.

Sellers' Market, Phase II

This is the riskiest phase of all in the market cycle.

You can spot the very beginning of this phase because properties and space begin to stay on the market longer. Gone are the days when multiple offers are presented to properties the instant they hit the market. Office and retail space is getting filled up, but not snatched up.

Sellers and *lessors* (who have space to lease) are still getting inflated prices, but they're waiting longer for buyers and *lessees* (who need space) to act. Land is still being purchased for speculation. The amount of construction in the pipeline begins to look excessive.

For the first time since the Buyers' Market, Phase II stage began, business and job growth begin to slow.

As investors sniff that the market is changing, they again conclude that now is the peak, and it's time to sell those properties. Suddenly there is much more space on the market, exceeding what can be absorbed.

The overcorrection continues and even more properties come on the market. As it takes longer to move them, sellers lower their prices. Building owners who are feeling the effects of an office-space glut begin to slash lease rates.

You know what happens from here—history repeats itself. The downward spiral picks up speed as each owner and seller reaches his personal panic threshold and caves in to get the deal done.

Smart investors have long since pulled their money out of this market and have already bought into another emerging market. They did this as soon as their leading indicators hinted that the market was transitioning into a Sellers' Market, Phase II.

Remember the two main market forces that will tip you off to this transition: The first is job growth. When it becomes stagnant, that means there are no more people moving into the area. Demand for properties is about to fall. Unless an area can create more jobs, it will begin an inevitable downward phase.

The second main market force to watch constantly is supply. In every emerging market, a key factor causing that market to lose its momentum is overbuilding and oversupply. When builders build more than demand warrants, they're forced to lower their prices and sell inventory to pay the bank notes that are marching due.

The Market Cycle and Land Use

The commercial real estate value cycle can be measured in three ways: growth, maturity, and decline.

Growth Phase

During this stage, there is an abundance of rural land, usually being used as farmland. It sits on the outskirts of existing urban areas. As urban activity picks up, land becomes scarce and expensive.

Development pushes out to the rural areas, where land can be bought at lower prices. These areas attract urban dwellers who are priced out of the market. They now can pay less for the land, and the farmers receive more than they would by keeping it as farmland.

As development continues, local governments show their support by creating additional infrastructure, such as roads, water and sewer lines, schools, and police and fire departments. The infrastructure is expensive, but hey, the market is going like gangbusters. Besides, governments fund these improvements from all the tax revenues that the developments create.

Mature Phase

This occurs when much of the available land in an area is now developed and growth begins to slow. As the area matures, other sections of the new fringe become the next growth targets.

Development during the mature phase consists of identifying spare lots of land called *infill areas* and transforming them into their highest and best use. Some parcels may become residential, others will be retail centers to support that new population, and other parts will be zoned for office buildings or industrial space.

During the mature phase, an opportunity presents itself to revitalize some of the original buildings that were built during the early part of the growth period.

Decline Phase

Local governments become stretched. Their focus is out on the fringe, building infrastructure and creating new tax bases farther and farther from the city center. Often money will be raised from taxpayers in the mature areas, only to find it redirected to infrastructure needs in the growth areas. The cities become hooked on growth. Now the mature areas begin to look threadbare, as repairs are deferred. This marks the beginning of the decline phase.

Don't invest your money in areas going through the decline phase. It takes too long for governments not only to recognize the decline, but to get around to doing something about it. The time to invest in such areas, as I said earlier, is when governments put their money where their plans are, and actually begin projects and development incentives to revitalize the blighted areas.

We are currently purchasing a property on the south side of Dallas, where the city has committed to $73 million in incentives for developers to revitalize the area. We will reposition the property to a more upscale one, while other developers are buying older properties that they will tear down and replace with high-end retail, entertainment, and commercial spaces.

The entire area is destined to become an alternative to the very desirable *Uptown* area of Dallas. Young urban professionals who are priced out of Uptown will view this area as the next best viable alternative, as an entire *work-live-play* area is created.

WHAT DRIVES DEMAND IN A MARKET

The first demand factor in any market is the local and national economy. Despite what the national media would like you to believe, most economies are driven by local job growth. Nevertheless, the *perception* of what the national economy is doing can help or hinder local trends.

Take any real estate market and you'll find investors who fall into one of three groups: the seasoned professionals, the rank amateurs, and everyone in between.

Earlier in this chapter we discussed how the pros read a market and act long before the crowd even knows what's going on. The rank amateurs and a good hunk of investors in between (that third group) do not get their information from hard data on market trends.

No, they get it from Fox News, CNN, a couple of blogs they follow, and lots of gossip. Therefore, when the national media does feature stories about all the new real estate millionaires being minted each week, the amateurs sit up and pay attention. When these investors sit on a plane or in a taxi and hear someone brag about how his cousin just made a fortune in condo developments, the amateurs start to salivate. And finally, when they go out to dinner and the waitress reveals that she, too, is a real estate investor, it's time to *get in while the getting is good!*

That's also the time when the professionals are selling like bandits and hightailing it out of that market.

Of course, the opposite is also true. The pros move into a market when the *gloom factor* is at its peak, judging by headlines, news stories, foreclosure auctions, and taxi talk.

Other than that powerful psychological factor, it usually doesn't matter what is happening in the national economy. As we already discussed, the local job growth and supply situations are much more important than the national headlines.

Demographics are also a big predictor of demand in a market. The two big demographic trends happening in many markets right now are the rise of immigrants and the emergence of *echo boomers*, who are the children of *baby boomers*.

Over the next 50 years the immigrant population in the United States is expected to account for 62 percent of population growth. With that growth, you will see retail and apartments competing for these tenants.

Most first-generation immigrants spend long hours working to provide a better life for their families. They want their descendants to have a level of education and life that they didn't have. It's common for the first generation to live most of their lives in rental housing. The second generation is more likely to own homes.

With a major wave of immigrants coming to this country for the next 30 years, that means a wave of renters is also coming.

Keep an eye on the echo boomers. Their numbers are just starting to be felt in housing, as they are reaching the age when they can rent and spend. According to the United States Census Bureau, there will be 84.9 million echo boomers by 2010, and they're spenders. Investors who cater to their tastes in real estate will do nicely.

What Drives Supply

The flip side of demand is supply. Demand creates a market, but it's lack of supply that eventually levels off a market. When demand begins to shift and new populations come into an area, supply is usually abundant because of the excessive building of the previous emerging phase.

As all that supply gets absorbed, market prices begin to rise and demand grows for goods and services. Builders, retail outlets, and office spaces expand into the area to meet that demand, and supply once again begins to increase.

Because supply is such a critical factor for you to focus on, let's look at a few key things that influence it.

Land-Use Changes

Most cities and towns have zoning ordinances that restrict what you can build and where you can build it. For instance, if an area is zoned for industrial use, that's what you are limited to. The same goes for areas of the city that are zoned for commercial or residential use.

Some parts of a city may be zoned for both commercial and residential, and perhaps even for industrial as well. That gives you choices about how you can improve a property.

It's common to drive down a main road and see houses on each side. Then, at a larger intersection, you will find gas stations, dough-nut shops, and strip malls. Residential and commercial spaces inter-twine with each other as the need for both arises, and as local residents state their preferences for commerce through their buying decisions.

Moratoria

Sometimes a city will realize that too much of one type of property is adversely affecting the balance of properties. A *moratorium* may not be too far behind, which limits or bans further growth in that property type.

In the mid 2000s, an enormous number of apartment complexes were converted to condominiums in San Diego. The market for resi-dential housing was going through the roof. The average price for a single-family home became way out-of-reach for the average wage earner. For these people, the American Dream of home ownership became unaffordable.

The best alternative was condominiums, which were generally priced 20 to 30 percent below the average price of a single-family home. Demand increased—quickly.

Developers were buying apartment complexes, making a few changes, and then selling the individual units off as condos. They made so much money that—of course—more developers got into the game and more apartments came off the market to become condos.

Not only did the supply of apartments become converted to con-dos, but builders did not replenish the apartment supply. They were too busy building new condos. Rents shot up for the remaining apart-ment units, making them unaffordable for many lower-paid workers.

When this happened, San Diego put a moratorium on condo conversions. This eventually rebalanced the housing stock, but in the meantime, prices for condos went that much higher.

Cities have been known to put moratoria on land use, septic hook-ups, and a variety of real estate building types, depending on the local imbalances. This is one more reason to stay on top of activities at the local economic development office.

Obsolescence

It may be possible for cathedrals and other special structures to be just fine after hundreds of years. However, most commercial properties have an average useful life, regardless of how well they're cared for. When they exceed that useful life, their value begins to decline.

For instance, an office building that was built many years ago will not be wired up for today's Internet needs. That makes it unusable for many companies. Some buildings can be retrofitted at reasonable expense, but others cannot.

The same is true with outdated *HVAC*, or *heating/ventilation/air-conditioning/cooling*. Competing properties get built with the latest energy-saving and comfort amenities, while older buildings either must charge lower rents or steadily lose occupancy.

There comes a point when owners can't afford the upgrades, but can't afford to run an empty building, either. They sell at a steep discount to someone who now will own the property at a much lower cost basis. With some creative financing and rehab work, the new owners may be able to breathe new life into the property.

Eminent Domain

A city sometimes decides that it needs a large parcel of land for a new highway, convention center, or other major project. The forced-taking of a large area can sometimes cause a big change in the supply of a particular property type.

The same holds true for large areas that are condemned, which occurred in parts of New Orleans after Hurricane Katrina. Forward-thinking investors can sometimes anticipate the effects of these sudden shifts and act quickly, thus either preserving their investments or creating new opportunities.

AMATEUR MISTAKE: "I'LL WAIT UNTIL THE MARKET CHANGES BEFORE I JUMP IN."

A great many investors fall into what I call the *local paradigm*. Here's how it works:

The commercial market starts to recover and prices rise. Investors look at the opportunities on the market and kick themselves—they could have bought these same properties six months ago for 20 to 30 percent less.

They put off buying a property until the market *corrects*, and prices come down to where they *should be*. Unfortunately for them, the market simply continues its upward climb.

Another six months go by and prices are up another 20 to 30 percent. These investors now exclaim to anyone who will listen: "These buyers are crazy! I've lived in this market all my life and I can tell you—nobody will buy commercial real estate in this area for those prices!"

They continue to stay on the sidelines. And—you got it—prices continue to climb.

When these local experts endure this self-kicking two or three more times, they finally throw in the towel and *go with the flow*. They, too, buy into the market.

Only now they've waited so long that they truly are buying at the top. By definition, *the top* is when there's the greatest amount of positive news to report, and it took that much news to convince these people.

Don't let this happen to you. Make sure you are guided by facts and research, and not by any decades-old impressions of the market that you've known since you were a kid.

I'm often asked, "When is a good time to buy commercial real estate?" I answer "*Now*—if you are buying the right property type, in the right emerging market, at the right price." That's a much more accurate and useful answer than "Oh, the right time is one year from now," without qualifying the statement.

Putting Your Ear to the Railroad Track: How to Know the Profit Train Is Coming Before Others Do

The profit train will give you clear signals, if you know what to listen for.

The first very clear signal will come in the form of job growth. I'm not talking about Don's Donuts hiring two cashiers; I mean that you must watch for announcements that substantial jobs are moving in.

At one point, Countrywide Mortgage announced that it would move its headquarters and 9,000 jobs from California to Dallas, Texas. At about the same time, Fidelity Investments in Boston announced that it would transfer 1,500 jobs from Boston to Dallas.

When you hear such things about a market, your next step should be to call the Chamber of Commerce in the lucky market. Ask what other jobs are coming into the market and what the city is doing to attract these jobs.

Strong leadership in a city will entice corporations to come into an area by doing a combination of four things:

1. **Tax abatements.** The city will give a tax break to a commercial property owner. At one point, Cleveland offered a 75-percent tax abatement for 12 years. In other words, if you renovated a commercial property in the city, you would not need to pay 75 percent of your taxes for 12 years. Apparently that wasn't sufficient to attract enough business to Cleveland, so they increased it to 100 percent for 15 years. That did the trick!
2. **Low-interest loans.** These entice businesses because their debt service expenses are reduced.
3. **Free money.** Dallas is providing $73 million in incentive funds for anyone willing to take part in the redevelopment of the Oak Cliffs area.
4. **Free or very-low-cost land.** This gives corporations an opportunity to move their headquarters or build an auto plant for costs that are way under the market. San Antonio created a

land package for Toyota so that it would build a manufacturing plant and create 8,000 new jobs.

When you understand what a city is doing to attract new businesses, you can gauge how strong the job growth may be.

By the way, the Chamber of Commerce loves to speak to us investors. They know the only way to turn the city around relatively quickly is to have us come in and invest.

Here's another good indication that you've found a prime area to invest—new *big-box retail* stores being built in the area. Is Home Depot, Best Buy, or Wal-Mart establishing a presence in the market? If so, you can bet these outfits did some heavy-duty research and that there is an economic resurgence going on in that area.

Key Factors

You already know how critical job growth is to the economic vitality of an area. When jobs are coming into a market, it usually takes the form of relocations at first. Those attractive economic incentives we just discussed are enough to cause major employers to decide: "This area is for us." Relocations can also be a fairly quick *shot in the arm.*

Job growth then happens in the form of new hiring in the local market. After that headquarters was relocated to the market, all the support infrastructure—the markets, shops, gas stations, and so on—will grow to meet that sudden demand.

As demand for workers increases, the supply of workers drops. This leads to an increase in median income. This good news will in turn attract new retailers to the area, and more jobs are created. Aren't upward spirals great?

Population trends is another key factor. People move for a variety of reasons and they move in waves. In the early 2000s, a wave of people moved from cold-weather states, such as in New England, down to Florida. Then, as prices rose in Florida, part of this wave was priced out of that market.

Not wanting to go all the way back to New England, they stopped halfway back, in the Carolinas. They even have a name: *halfbacks*. As home prices increased even more in Florida, the number of halfbacks grew. The Carolinas enjoyed an economic resurgence, largely because of these halfbacks.

There is also the *global effect*. I don't mean global warming, but Global moving vans! They are a good indication of where people are going. If you find out where Global or other major van lines have a high percentage of one-way trips, it is sure to be an area where in-migration is happening.

Watch for whether road crews are out widening roads that lead to an area. Those big projects only happen when master plans indicate major growth. Get a list from the state department of transportation for future projects. Few, if any, of your competitors will know to do this.

Areas with state government offices and also universities are often strong, enduring markets.

After all, governments are very slow to lay off workers. They provide a steady source of jobs. Even after an election year, a bunch of people move out only to be replaced by a bunch of the winning candidate's people.

The same holds true for universities. With the echo boomers now coming into the college ranks, we have a surge of new students. Many juniors and seniors are dying to live on their own in apartments. They also spend freely at retail shops and restaurants that cater to them.

More Local Clues of Upcoming Strong Markets

Demographics

We've already discussed many demographic factors, but here are some more key considerations.

Each commercial property must attract its own target demographic profile in order to be successful. Depending on the type of commercial property, they could include: number of businesses, customers, or families in an area; size of those entities; median income; age; ethnic makeup; and so on.

A professional *demographer* will analyze an area by drawing three rings on a map of the property and its market. The rings are drawn at a one-mile, three-mile, and five-mile radius around the property.

As an owner, you should know the demographic makeup within each of these rings. A restaurant owner may have a great chef, the best food, and award-winning décor, but if the right consumers for his food are not found within that three-mile ring, he's looking at a real uphill climb.

An apartment owner might have an option to buy a *Class B* property for a great price. The property is in good repair and the numbers look fine. But if the income level has dropped for residents within that three-mile radius, that's probably the reason why the price is so attractive. That property will be harder—not impossible, but much harder—to fill. Because 80 percent of apartment tenants come from within a three-mile radius of the property, this sudden income shift may now mean that they cannot afford your B rents.

Apartments will not be the only commercial properties affected by this lower income. The area may no longer be able to support higher-end retail and restaurants. As leases come due, Target stores may be replaced by Dollar stores. This is a sign that the economics are worsening and you are definitely not on the *path of progress*. Values will suffer.

Traffic Count

All commercial properties are concerned with traffic count. How many potential customers are going by every day? How many eyeballs will see the property signage? Different types of retail stores need different minimum traffic counts to be successful, unless they have a large component of Internet sales, or they are particularly good at marketing. Very few are.

You can get traffic counts from the local city government, which should be collecting this data regularly. Compare previous traffic counts with the current ones to discover any trends. If it's going down, is it because population is leaving the area, or because new roads have opened up, thus taking the traffic away? Study these numbers and formulate your questions. Then talk with the economic development people and your own network of brokers and property managers to get the answers.

Traffic Flow

Determine which way the traffic flows at different times of the day. Is it local traffic, or people passing through as part of their commute? What about future plans of the transportation department: Is there a chance they will widen the roads in the future? If so, try to judge how that will affect your traffic flow, including the ability of traffic to come in and out of your site.

School Districts

This is an extremely important factor when you plan to own apartments. Some school districts are far better than others. Many parents are drawn to districts that will give their kids the best education.

In fact, a school district can make or break a property. If you have a nice *A* property in an inferior school district, it will be much harder to keep it fully occupied at *A-level* rents. The bad school district is enough reason for *A* tenants to move out or never move in, and they have the money available to enjoy multiple rental options.

We own a property where the school district runs right down the center of the property! Children in one part of the complex go to a different school from kids a few feet away in the other part of the complex. When there are vacancies in *front* units (the better school district), parents will frequently ask to be moved there.

Access

This factor can cause problems for an otherwise great location. If you can see a property from the highway and it gets a huge daily traffic count, you're halfway there. If drivers cannot figure out how to get to your property, you will lose a great deal of business.

I own a Class A property in Brownsville, Texas. There is only one other A property in the market. My property has the best location because you can access it easily from the highway. My competitor is highly visible, but no one can figure out how to get to him! What a shame.

If people can't get to a property, they quickly get frustrated and stop trying. I've got another property in a different market: It can be reached from three different directions, but there is no one *easy way*. We have to market extra hard to keep the property full, and that cuts into my profits. It's been an expensive lesson that I have now thoroughly mastered—and am handing to you!

By the way, just because you have a property located at an intersection, do not assume it is a great site. You must watch for problems entering and exiting that property, including backed-up traffic at the intersection. Even when you see an open path, you must first check with the city and sometimes state (if it's a state highway) to make sure there are no restrictions on turning off and onto that road.

In the Next Chapter

If you've been paying attention, you now know more than a great many commercial investors who simply follow the crowd, and end up buying properties in mediocre markets, or worse.

Once you've identified some good markets, the next step is to get your deal-attraction engine humming, so that you see opportunity after opportunity in those markets and can *cherry-pick* the best. That's what the next chapter is about.

Don't Listen to the Crowd

Today, Grand Central Station in New York City is beautiful. However, in the 1970s, it was a different situation altogether. The area was in the midst of serious decay. It was crummy, run-down, and a destination point for no one except those entering and leaving the city as quickly as they possibly could.

The old Commodore Hotel next to Grand Central was in big trouble. It was a disgraceful sight. I knew that the neighborhood was ready for a change, and acquiring the Commodore Hotel became a quest.

Even my father couldn't believe I was serious. He said "buying the Commodore at a time when even the Chrysler Building is in bankruptcy is like fighting for a seat on the Titanic."

I had to structure an extremely complex deal with other interested parties. It took several years to negotiate everything. I still needed to get financing. I hired a real estate broker who had a lot of experience, and who was in his sixties. I was only 27 years old at the time, and having a mature, accomplished presence with me worked to my advantage.

I bought the Commodore for $10 million, with $6 million going to the city for back taxes. I then sold the hotel to the city for one dollar, and they leased it back to me for 99 years.

Now, people and critics love this building. It started the revitalization of the Grand Central area and opened in 1980 to great success. Today, it's a hub of New York City—thriving and beautiful.

Donald Trump with Meredith McIver, *Never Give Up* (John Wiley & Sons, 2008, page 62).

3

How to Become a
Deal Magnet

 AMATEUR MISTAKE: "I CAN'T DO REAL ESTATE BECAUSE I DON'T HAVE THE TIME TO CHASE DEALS."

This is one of the top two issues that stop 90 percent of would-be investors dead in their tracks. (The other issue: *I don't have the money.* We'll get to that one later.)

There are two key principles you must know in order to *break the time barrier*:

The First Time Principle: You Have More Time than You Think

Stay with me here: I'm not asking you to work harder or get less sleep. You might already be stretched pretty thin. I know I was when I started out. But in my experience, when most people say "I don't have the time," what they mean is "I choose to spend my time on other things versus this new project and I don't know whether it will pay off."

Let me put it a different way: Let's say you are totally frazzled these days. You don't get enough sleep, don't have much fun, and can't get all your work done. Sound like anyone you know?

Now imagine that you knew with certainty that your Great Great Uncle Ebenezer buried a substantial treasure chest in your family's backyard 122 years ago. You found some old parchment hidden in the attic with only the general location. Would you make the time to go digging around under cover of darkness? That's a no-brainer. Why? Because it met two key tests: The reward was substantial, and the process was straightforward.

The rewards from commercial real estate can be as large as you like. You already know that from looking at Donald Trump. The sticking point is the believability that you, too, can follow the process.

That's why the trick with real estate investing is to put in as *little time as possible* up front into key investing activities until you see for yourself that your labor is paying off.

Later in this chapter I show you multiple great sources for deals. But there's no point skipping ahead to them if we don't get *the time thing* straightened out first.

I don't care if you're the President of the United States—you can shave off 20 minutes here and 30 minutes there, a few times a week, for things you really want to do. You could be an air traffic controller at O'Hare Airport and still have a bit of time during the day to put toward your chosen activity. You simply need to want it enough, or pressures and excuses will squash your plans. That's where Old Ebenezer's treasure comes in. *You make time for the important things.*

When I started investing in real estate, I had a busy one-man landscaping business and a house-cleanout business. By the time I got back to my one-bedroom apartment at night, I was absolutely beat. But I knew there was treasure buried out there, in the form of small properties that would throw off cash.

I discovered how to do direct mail campaigns. At night, exhausted in front of the TV, I would stuff and stamp envelopes. I simply did as many as I could before falling asleep.

I started to see some leads this way. I was slowly getting more calls, and some of those turned into appointments. A few of these leads actually became deals. I had proven to myself that working this way was leading me to part of the treasure waiting for me out there.

On Sundays I would grab the newspaper and go right to the classifieds. I looked for commercial property for sale. At first I just got familiar with the ads. I then called the ads that caught my eye.

Please understand that at first I was *lousy* at this. I bumbled around. But so what! I was never again going to see those property owners advertising in the paper anyway. Besides, I didn't invade their home; it was they who ran the ad. I was polite when I called up, so I just persisted until it got easier. And it did.

In fact, I was surprised at how friendly most of the sellers were. They were happy to talk with me. After a few more calls, I was even more surprised at how good I got at talking to them. A little experience goes a long way. Eventually I got a few deals from this approach. Now I had two things going for me: direct mail and calling a few sellers.

Note that both these activities were highly flexible: If I had a bit more time one day, I licked more stamps or called more sellers. Other days I could barely do any. But I kept it up, and *didn't let excuses get in the way of my dreams.*

I would also attend the local real estate club once a month. I remember my friend Al telling me how he kept getting deals from this one particular broker. The broker gave Al first crack at any deal that came up. I thought, *Wow how lucky is he!*

I asked Al how he got this broker to give him deals. He said that he had a great relationship with the guy, but it didn't happen overnight. Al was patient and just kept watering and tending this seed until it took root and eventually became a strong tree—one that was giving him money-fruit regularly.

I thought, if even *Al* could do it, *I* could do it. I began to look really closely at those ads. I noticed which brokers were in the paper a lot. I started calling them and eventually took a few out to lunch. Before long I had three brokers giving me deals on a regular basis.

Yes, all this was a pain. I could have been watching the Red Sox lose more games (this was well before they became regular champions). I could have slept in on Sunday morning. I even had to plan my landscaping jobs so I could clean myself up and take the brokers to lunch. But I also could see that strong-box of Ebenezer's out there, waiting for me to unearth it! Pretty soon the cashier's checks from deal after deal were enough to motivate me *big time*.

The Second Time Principle: Getting Started in Real Estate Investing Takes Less Time than You Might Think

You do *not* have to come home after work, change your clothes and hit the streets, knocking on doors. You do *not* have to bang the phones every night, calling dozens of ads. What you do have to put in place is an agreement with yourself to invest a small amount of time regularly, until you start to see movement toward your goals.

Notice I said "*Getting started in* real estate investing. . . ." Once you're rolling with a deal or two in different stages of completion, of course it will take more time. But you'll be so excited with the prospect of a deal paying off that you'll easily make the time at that point.

The major mistake most real estate gurus make is to urge people to carve out many hours per week for real estate, right from the get-go. That's an unrealistic expectation, doomed to failure.

So start out making forward motion every day on the key, high-payoff activities I'm about to show you.

Don't Chase Deals—*Attract* Them

You shouldn't be like the dog, chasing his tail, getting worn out, and never quite reaching his goal. The real professionals attract deals.

This is not simply a choice of different words: It's an extremely powerful marketing concept.

Think what happens when you bang the phones and knock on doors: You're faced with enormous amounts of rejection. You may get a polite "No thanks," or you may get a "Get the %$#*@ off my porch, you %$#*@." A friend of mine has had guns pulled on him and was chased down the street by a junkyard dog.

You may say: *No problemo, Dave, I'm tough. I can handle it.*

No you can't. Sooner or later it will wear away your insides and you'll find the path of least resistance. You'll convince yourself that commercial real estate doesn't work, or it's not the right time in your market. Those are just variations on the old *My Dog Ate My Homework* set of excuses.

I can't really blame these failed investors, because they went about it the wrong way. When you have marketing systems that allow you only to hear from motivated sellers, your life is far more pleasant.

What you do is put out the word that you're looking for real estate, and the only responses you get are from the people who are at least somewhat motivated.

Don't get me wrong: You still will talk to a lot of tire-kickers. They may *want* to sell now, but do not yet *need* to sell. That's okay. The key thing is they called you.

Even the few calls you may make to classified ads are in this category. After all, you didn't make them put the ad in the paper. They wanted people to call them.

When you make small but consistent efforts in attracting sellers through proven marketing techniques, you're not on a breathless sprint to failure, but on a sustainable path to wealth.

An Easy Way to Recognize the Motivated Seller

Even if you get a certain number of duds contacting you, it's still possible to be highly efficient with your time and find the gems.

The trick is to recognize quickly when you have a mere tire-kicker and when you have a real prospect. All you have to do is ask three questions:

Questions 1 & 2: "How Much Are You Asking for Your Property?"...
Followed Quickly by "How Did You Determine That Price?"

If sellers say they are looking for the current market price, you simply explain that you are an investor. That means you can act very quickly, but need to buy below market price so you can resell at the market.

Why would anyone sell for a below-market price? Trust me—it happens all the time. Many people just want to be rid of a problem property that's been plaguing them for a long time. They're psychologically done with that property and now want to be physically done with it.

Other people are in a big rush because they're moving to a new city, or need cash quickly, or a nasty divorce just happened. Whatever the reason, you want to be that buyer at the right place at the right time.

When you ask "How did you determine that price?" a few may say: "Look, Mister, that's what I paid for it and I just want my money back." This would be a promising response from your perspective.

Are you *taking advantage* of these people? No. Remember, they called you. You're helping them out of a tough situation. In fact, they will usually thank you afterwards. In my experience, most sellers don't actually lose money in my transactions. They instead are selling for below market, but their equity in the property allows them to do that.

Question 3: How Fast Are You Looking to Sell?

If they say they have time and are in no big hurry, this usually means they want to put their property on the market and let investors compete for it. These are not profitable deals. Rarely have I won in a situation when I competed directly against other investors. That's because other investors are usually willing to pay more for a property than I am.

Tell the seller: "I can close very quickly and work well with sellers who need to close quickly. . . . But if you have time to market your property to the highest bidder, then I probably am not your buyer. Is this your situation?"

You'll get the answer you need after you ask that question.

In my living room is a bright-green sequined frog. I got it in the Cincinnati airport. It's a reminder that I became successful in commercial real estate because I was willing to kiss a lot of frogs. They're also known as *unmotivated sellers*.

I still kiss these frogs today, by spending a moment asking them these three questions. Sure enough, some of these frogs turn into princely deals!

A Simple and Inexpensive Way to Start Seeing Deals Immediately

As I hinted earlier, one of the fastest ways to get your deal-attraction machine cranking is to do direct mail.

Yes, we all consider it junk mail, but no, we *don't* all throw it away. If we did, then those very smart and very rich companies would have long ago stopped sending us credit card offers.

The stuff works—if it's done correctly. Most business owners are incompetent at using direct mail, then blame their failure on the tool, and not on themselves. Hey, that's fine with me. It thins the herd.

Even when direct mail is done right, it's still a numbers game. Depending on the offer and many other factors, you might only get 1 response out of 100 letters. That's okay, because that lousy one percent can make you very wealthy.

If you're reliably getting a response, then you can ramp up your mailing. Now when you send 1,000 letters, you'll maybe get ten people to call you. Of those callers, perhaps only two to three will be serious sellers. That's also okay, because one single deal can make you a lot of money. It will more than pay for the hundreds or thousands of letters that didn't generate a response.

What Is a Good Response Rate?

I get that question all the time. The response rate doesn't matter: It all comes down to your *return on investment*, also known as your *ROI*.

If you had a 100 percent response from all your letters, but never did a deal, I would call that a lousy ROI. On the other hand, let's say you only get one reply for 1,000 letters. That's a one-tenth of a percent response rate. But say that deal brings you $35,000 in profits. I'd say your ROI is pretty good!

Consider the Source

The source of your list is one very important factor in your direct-mail success. Go to your city assessor's office, where all the tax rolls are kept. By law, much of that information is open to public view. Ask for a list of all commercial property owners.

Sometimes the assessor's office will give you a difficult time about getting the list. You might be the first person to have asked in a long time, or your request means extra copying work for someone. Be extra friendly but persistent. In my experience, most people at these offices around the country are very friendly and have a helpful attitude.

Sometimes the office won't provide you with the list, but will refer you to a list broker. These people make their livelihood from maintaining lots of mailing lists for practically anything.

When I have a choice, I like to get my list from the assessor's office because it is the most current.

I recently had a call from a student who was looking for help to analyze an office deal. She had sent out her first direct mail campaign and was surprised at the amount of response she got. She not only had an interested seller for an office building but sellers for two apartment complexes as well.

Some areas respond better than others, just as some letters work better than others. The keys to success are to keep mailing, and tweak your mailings until you find success. Try a different headline, use some local news item in the letter to make it clear you're a local investor, and so on.

Sometimes I'll ask a list broker to find people who have owned their properties for 20 years or more. These people have used a large portion of their depreciation and may be looking to sell. They may also be close to retirement age and just want to move on.

The thing I like about list brokers is you can ask them for certain criteria in your list and tell them that you only want to pay for those criteria and they will get just such a list for you. It really is pretty scary how much information is out there on all of us.

The list is priced on a per-name basis. Don't go hog-wild and rent many thousands of names. Just start with a few hundred or a few thousand, and see how things go.

Note that I said *rent* a name. You typically cannot mail to these people more than once. How will they know you mailed multiple times? They *seed the list* with fake names and monitor what gets mailed to those names. If you're caught, you've breached the contract you signed. Not good.

As you do more deals, you should consider asking the broker to give you only names of owners with properties above a certain size. My cutoff usually is properties with assessed values of $2 million or more. That weeds out a lot of properties that I'm no longer interested in buying. That's just fine with me at this stage. You might want to start somewhat smaller.

Here's another tip: Every letter should have a headline. When owners open your letter, there should be a big, effective headline beckoning them to read on. The sole purpose of that headline is to sell the reader on reading the letter.

Because of this, your headline should state the biggest benefit that owners will get from selling their property to you. For instance, the following headline has worked for me through the years:

I want to Buy Your Boston Commercial Property

Naturally I change the name of the city to the appropriate location for whatever owners I'm targeting.

One thing I was surprised to discover about letters is some people keep them for a long time. Maybe they're not interested in selling at this moment, but they file the letter away because they're mulling over in their heads the idea of selling, which I might have planted.

Letters are easy and inexpensive and will get your phone ringing in a very short time.

The Magic That Happens When Your Deal Pipeline Is Full

Letters are only one way to get deals. Before I go into others, let me tell you about the evolution you'll experience when you start to attract leads.

After you read this book—and maybe even before you're done—you'll want to do a deal as soon as you can.

You will start to look at deals and analyze numbers. Soon you'll find a deal that just might work. That's when you need to be careful: In your eagerness, you may stop analyzing it dispassionately, and start wanting to *make the deal work.*

You'll say to yourself "Hey, this market is bound to be stronger than it is today, so I think I can boost rents just a little." You may shade the occupancy numbers a bit higher, too. When you find yourself doing this . . . STOP! It's not a good deal.

When you have a full pipeline, you won't try to improve on the numbers. You'll be confident that another deal is right around the corner. In fact, you'll be constantly reviewing them, and the challenge is not to find more deals, but to narrow them down to fewer. That's a great position to be in. By the way, when you have that kind of confidence, it shows! Sellers sense you're confident and that you mean it when you make them an offer and say: "That's the best I can do."

I got an e-mail from a broker the other day. He said he has a three-property portfolio that's not listed on the market. I can have it before others see it. I looked into it and the numbers were a bit high for a property built in the 1970s.

I e-mailed him back and told him so. He replied that there was lots of upside potential (that's a favorite response among brokers). Well, that may be true, but with my deal pipeline full, I can afford to wait for the deals that have proven numbers, and not potential numbers.

You must do the same, even if you don't have as big a pipeline as I do—yet. Do not get into a deal for the sake of having a deal.

The Secret To Finding Deals

Real estate is a relationship business. Your business becomes a real self-sustaining operation when you have a network of contacts and specialists with whom you do deal after deal. You all win that way, because each time it becomes easier and more profitable.

In a later chapter I explain how to surround yourself with your *Dream Team* of specialists. And later in this chapter I describe ten great sources for deals. But I need to prepare you first by laying out three Key Rules for Doing Business with Just About Anyone.

Let me put it to you plainly: I don't care what else you have going for you—if you follow these rules, you'll be successful. If you don't, just go back to whatever day job you have, because you won't cut it in commercial real estate.

Rule 1: Always Do What You Say You Will Do

Sounds simple, right? Then why is it most people don't follow the rule?

It's because they are much better at making excuses than keeping commitments.

You should be slow to make commitments, but when you make one, move heaven and earth to keep it. You will surprise and delight your business associates when you do that, and word will get around. They'll want to work with you, because your deals will be some of the very few they can count on.

Rule 2: Make Doing Business with You Easy

It's another rule that seems so common sense but is so uncommon in practice.

Look for opportunities to make the other person's life easier.

- Does she need help setting up the appraisal, meeting an inspector, or getting paperwork signed off?
- If she's waiting on a check from you, consider wiring the money so it's there instantly instead of waiting for the mail to arrive and for the check to clear.
- Is she short-handed in some way? Think creatively about how you can help to get some of her tasks done.

It's all about exceeding expectations and then becoming a topic of conversation. She may then tell her friend: "You won't believe what just happened; I had to slog over to meet the inspector at this property, and Dave actually volunteered to do it for me! That's the first time a buyer has ever volunteered to do that!"

It's not about thinking what's your job and what's the seller's job. It's instead about thinking what jobs does the seller have that you could help with. Are you required to do it? No. Are you even expected to do it? No. But it's just those situations where your doing the task will impress the daylights out of the other person.

I am not suggesting that you become the errand-boy for the other party. I'm suggesting that you look for ways to distinguish yourself and stand out from the competition. Following this rule is one of the fastest ways to do so.

Rule 3: Don't Be a Pain in the Butt

Some investors like to negotiate every little point, thinking they're impressing others by being tough negotiators. Other investors do so because they're just cheap. Either way, it's a great method for doing single deals with people who will never want to work with you again.

Why? There are plenty of other investors and life is too short to be nickel-and-dimed to death, especially if you're selling something of value.

Let's say a *primo* deal is up for sale. The seller calls an experienced broker and asks to have the property put on the market. However, the seller doesn't want to go through the circus of putting it on the open market. He wants the broker to present it to a small group of people that the broker knows can close the deal.

Will the broker show it to the butt-pain investor, or to others who are a pleasure to do business with? Hmmm.

This scenario happens all the time. You want to be part of that inner circle to get these *off-market deals* presented to you first. There is potentially millions of dollars of profit in being on such inner-circle lists.

We just put a high-rise building under contract in Dallas. It came from an estate sale and the sellers wanted to move quickly. They also didn't want a lot of media attention. The deal was quietly presented to us and one other company. The other company had more experience buying high-rise properties. In fact, they were one of the largest commercial property owners and developers in Texas.

They *were* the stronger buyer. But we got the deal.

We had the carefully cultivated reputation of doing everything we can possibly do to make a deal easy for sellers and brokers. We also had the advantage of being smaller and nimbler. After my business partner and I went to the site for an inspection, we made an offer on the spot. The other company? They sent in acquisition guys who had to fill out a report . . . create a presentation . . . run it up the flagpole to the suits back at the corporate office . . . get the deal to the right committee. . . .

We snatched that deal off the table before our competition could even get their knife and fork in it.

Your reputation is absolutely key in the commercial world. Build a good one right from the start.

How to Have More Deals Than You Can Work On

It is systems that will keep that pipeline of yours full.

I'm not an engineer, but I sure do love systems. They've made me a great deal of money and they'll do the same for you. Systems work so well because you can set them up, then delegate them to other people.

They run the systems, and your job is to monitor and improve the whole thing.

I read a great book on systems when I started my real estate business. It's called the *E-myth Revisited*, by Michael Gerber.

The book talks about how to create systems so you are constantly working *on* your business instead of *in* your business. When you work on your business, you continually look for improvements. The goal is to make tomorrow work better than today. When you merely work in the business, you're so caught up in the daily grind, you can't step back and make adjustments. Tomorrow will be the same as today, except you'll be one day older.

When you make a mistake, create a system so you don't make it again. Determine what you do best and systemize everything else. Sure, you can't do that on Day One, but you should be working toward that goal from Day One.

Your marketing systems are a key component. For example, I have a mailing system. I buy lists of property owners to whom I want to send mail at least once per year. I hand that list to a bunch of little old ladies in a local elderly complex in my hometown.

I supply my ladies with my marketing letters, envelopes, and other needed materials.

I also give them a written explanation of which letter goes to which type of property owner in what month. When letters come back marked as non-deliverable, they take that owner's name off the list.

They call when they're running low on supplies and when the letters are ready to be mailed. Yes, they're wonderful little old ladies, but even so, I want to get the letters that are ready for mailing so I can drop them in the mail. Anyone who's been in direct mail for any length of time can tell you horror stories about money spent on mailing campaigns, only to find out that the letters never got mailed and the postage was stolen.

The best use of my time is to answer the phone when the seller calls. It's that simple. If I relied on myself to do the letter campaigns, it would just not get done. It's too easy to get busy and forget to get those letters out. Besides if you've ever stuffed, stamped, and written addresses on thousands of envelopes, you know that pretty soon it will be at the very bottom of your *to-do list*—the part you never get to.

You can go through the pain of creating your own systems, or you can simply find someone who's been down that road and created them already. That's the smart way to set up your business.

Successful People at First Make This Mistake

After you get and launch your marketing machine, you'll be talking with many sellers and doing deals regularly. You will reach the point where you have too many deals to handle. Your first temptation will be to turn off your buying machine.

Don't do it.

If you've ever been on a really large cruise ship, you know that it takes a very long time for the ship to get up to speed. That's the trade-off for having the power to cross an ocean. Your marketing machine is just like that cruise ship. It will take continuous effort by you and your team to get it up to cruising speed.

If you shut it off while you're busy with deals this month, the engine room will be stone cold by the time you realize two months from now that you're running low on new deals. Now you'll try to restart your marketing engine, but it will take another couple of months to get back up to speed again. You'll suffer in the meantime.

You are much better off keeping that pipeline full, and using your network to make you even more money: You can count on other investors not having well-oiled marketing machines. Most don't have a machine of any kind, and they're dying for new deals. So when you have one you just can't handle, go to your local real estate investing association. At the beginning of the meeting it's typical for people to stand up and describe the deals they have, deals they're looking for, and financing they need.

Wear a bright shirt or dress and give your one-minute description of a deal. Then stand in the back of the room and watch the investors come flocking. You can flip your leads to these people for some nice, quick, easy money.

Ten Sources For Great Deals

I cannot give you one marketing tool to get you ten deals—but I can easily give you ten marketing tools that will each get you one deal. Over time, you need to add all these techniques to your marketing system, and do them regularly.

Real Estate Brokers

People have mixed feelings about real estate brokers. Some say they'll try to sell you anything; others swear that they can't do business without brokers.

In my experience, once you have cultivated three or four good brokers in a given market, you'll have plenty of quality deals over time just from this one source.

When I started buying smaller commercial properties in Brockton, Massachusetts, years ago, I did just that: I made it my goal to cultivate three different brokers who were seeing most of the foreclosed properties in the area. These guys eventually fed me deal after deal, because I had followed the three relationship rules I gave you earlier: I did what I said I would do, I made their lives easier, and I was not a pain to work with.

I list brokers as the first great source because they really do have the potential to make you wealthy. Still, you must be selective, because some brokers are way better than others. (Isn't that the case with just about everything in life?)

Good brokers also try to cultivate buyers for two simple reasons: They figure these people may be buyers again, and they also want the commission when the buyers eventually want to sell.

Almost always it's a great idea to resell the property from the broker you bought it from, unless there were major problems. This will of course motivate him to bring you more deals.

Some investors try to save the commission by selling the property themselves on the Internet. What fools. Don't they realize they just burned their broker relationship in that town?

Cultivate your brokers not only with commissions from deals, but with good old rapport-building. What interests do they have? Send a newspaper clipping. What do you have in common? Talk about that on the next phone call. What kind of food do they like? Take them to lunch at a restaurant which serves that kind of food. Stay in touch and be a bright spot in their day. It's one of the highest-payoff activities you can do in this business.

Property Ownership Associations

Thinking about investing in a certain city? The first thing to do is join the local property owners association. Not only will you get a very good education, but you'll get to know the other owners in the city.

You'll discover how business is done in that city—and it does vary. You'll discover who are the good contractors, attorneys, property managers, and lenders. You will also get warnings about the little quirks that every city has ("Watch out about the Building Inspector—he's the Mayor's son-in-law"). This market intelligence will save you countless hours of frustration, not to mention big bucks.

A bonus comes from the relationship you create with the other owners. You will discover who buys what, and they'll learn what you like to buy. When the time comes to sell a property, they usually will tell the other members of the association first. You may get deals before they hit the market.

Want to get known by many members quickly? Become a leader in the association. The fastest way is to volunteer to be on the board or help the organization with events. The board members and the people who "made this all possible" are usually recognized at the beginning of each event. When you're named as one of them, you will find yourself moving to the inner circle of that organization.

Discover as much as you can about the members. First target members with whom you want to associate. Ask them if you could meet in their office for 20 minutes at a convenient time for them. Tell them you want to learn more about their business and how you could help them grow. One of the most powerful phrases is "What can I do for you?"

Genuinely attempt to help as many people as possible and it *will* come back to you, multiplied.

To help you get started in your search for groups, here are several national property owners associations:

- The Building Owners and Managers Association (www.boma.org)
- International Council for Shopping Centers (www.icsc.org)
- National Association of Apartment Owners (www.naahg.org)
- Institute for Real Estate Management (www.irem.org)

Start joining these groups, and look for local chapter meetings. They're loaded with solid information and good people to do business with.

Real Estate Investment Clubs

These clubs are similar to property owners associations but generally deal with smaller investors. There are great investment clubs all around the country; I've spoken at dozens of them.

Google your city for *real estate investment club/association* and the clubs in your area will pop up.

Get to know the operations by attending several meetings. Then to get the most out of your local club, you might inquire about starting a commercial real estate subgroup. That will put you in closer contact with like-minded people. Strange as it may seem, you'll find that these groups do not have a competitive atmosphere, but instead a cooperative one.

Attorneys

As good as you may get at real estate, you should always have one or more attorneys review your deals. It's their job to stay on top of changes in state and local laws. They also know how to rewrite contracts to be as much as possible in your favor.

There's another great reason to involve attorneys: They know a lot about changes in your local real estate market. Attorneys get involved when people file bankruptcy, when estates are liquidating property after someone's death, and when businesses are dissolving and foreclosures will occur.

Cultivate attorneys the same way that you cultivate real estate brokers. Then explain to them the sort of property you want to buy. If you follow my relationship principles and have some patience, you'll be privy to deals that never hit the market.

You can connect with attorneys through business organizations. Many active ones attend Chamber of Commerce and Rotary Club meetings. They are there to get more business, and so are you.

Also ask your growing network of brokers plus your pals at the real estate investing club. You'll start to hear the same names come up, and those are the best targets for cultivation.

Courthouse

Because many real-estate-related events are on the public record, your local courthouse is a good source for deals. There you will discover who has filed for bankruptcy, who is on schedule for foreclosure, the dates of sheriff's sales, and so on. Though many companies provide this information for a charge, I've found such services usually have stale information, to the tune of three to six weeks behind actual courthouse filings. That lag time gives your competition too much of an advantage.

Instead, consider taking a weekly trip to the courthouse and get the filings. Once you do it a couple of times, train someone else to do it for you. Remember—delegate, delegate, delegate.

Internet

Lazy investors use the Internet as an easy armchair source for deals. The only problem is the vast majority of deals on the Internet are garbage.

Using the Internet as your only source to find deals is like fishing without bait. You might get lucky and snag a fish, but you may die of hunger first.

Let's say a broker has a new listing for a strip mall. The first thing he'll do is look at his personal list of buyers to see who buys strip malls. Then he shows the deal to his top buyers. If they are not interested, he shows it to his entire list.

If none of his buyers is interested, he'll give the listing to the office manager to share with everyone in his office. They then show it to everyone on their lists. If none of their buyers is interested, this deal goes on the Internet and into the classified sections of the local newspaper.

If you simply take the convenient route of trolling the Internet for deals, you're pretty much staring at the bottom of the barrel.

There are exceptions, though: I got a commercial property in Austin, Texas, right from the Internet. I paid $8.6 million for it, and it appraised for $10.5 million. It's been a good deal.

Why do good deals occasionally show up on the Internet? It's because commercial brokers are not the only people who use it to market their deals. Property owners sometimes don't know a good broker, or don't want to work with any brokers. They'll hear that they can list a property right on the Internet, and that's what they do. The good deals usually originate in this way. My deal in Austin was from a seller in Minneapolis.

The granddaddy of all commercial property Internet sites is Loopnet. com. One of its membership levels is free. Another outfit is Costar.com. It is not cheap, so you'll find more serious investors on that site.

Direct Mail

I covered direct mail pretty thoroughly before, but I want to make a special point: Direct mail will eventually get you in front of many sellers with more than one property to sell. They just don't tell you that up front.

They want to make sure you are a player who actually comes through with your end of the deal. If you are and you do, as soon as you close your first deal with them, they'll often have another ready to go! Even if they don't have another one ready, when they are thinking of putting properties on the market down the road, they're likely to call you first to see if you are interested.

Government Agencies

From time to time, even Uncle Sam might be a deal source.

As you know, the government has many kinds of guarantee and subsidy programs to encourage commerce and growth. Sometimes these deals go bad and a government agency takes the property back, but doesn't want to own it forever. That's when they'll list the property for auction.

The Department of Housing and Urban Development (also known as *HUD*) sells commercial properties, among other types. One government site is www.homesales.gov. Even though it is called *homesales*, it also contains commercial property.

The U.S. Department of Agriculture sells similar real estate in rural areas. Its site is www.resales.usda.gov. If you monitor these sites regularly, you might find a solid deal.

Bank-Owned Properties

These types of properties are becoming quite widespread in our turbulent economy.

What you do is establish a relationship with the person in the bank who runs the *Real Estate Owned (REO) Department* or the *Loss-Mitigation Department*. She will have access to the bank's deals. Sometimes she'll not work with you directly, but will refer you to brokers whom she uses to sell the bank's properties. If you really work your way into the bank, it's possible to become the *go-to guy* even before the property goes to a broker.

These relationships do take time to develop. First go to your local savings and loan and ask these people if you could have 20 minutes of their time. Maybe take them out to lunch. Be prepared with a brief description of what you're looking for. Just be sure that you do not talk about *no-money-down* arrangements. Though it's definitely possible for you to get into a good property with none of your own money in the deal, mentioning *no money down* will brand you as an amateur and effectively end the conversation.

If you are patient and they eventually want to do business with you, it will be because they feel you can close and you have something in common with them.

These same people will negotiate *short sales* on properties the bank owns. That's when they'll sell the property for less than the mortgage amount. We recently got a commercial property short-saled from $4.3 million down to $2.6 million.

People You Meet

I was flying back from Panama and struck up a conversation with the guy sitting next to me. He was a commercial property developer. For the entire flight to Houston we talked about markets, strategies, and contacts, and he's now in my list of contacts.

Always be prepared with your *elevator speech*. That's a carefully crafted and memorized 30-second pitch to use when someone asks you what you do. You can then deliver it without thinking, and make it enticing enough for him to ask more questions.

When people ask me what I do, I tell them I invest in commercial properties in emerging markets throughout the United States. That gets them asking more questions. They become intrigued by what I do, because I believe that secretly most people want to be real estate investors. Only a small percentage actually take the time to discover what it takes to do it, the way you're doing right now.

After they've hit me with a few questions like "Where do you buy?" and "Do you travel a lot?" I always ask, "Whom do you know who might be looking to sell a commercial property?"

Occasionally they know someone who's in the market to sell. Most of the time they don't know anyone. That's okay, because I just put the seed in their head. I give them my card and ask them to call me in the future if something comes up.

I've gotten good referrals from asking that question and sometimes the phone call comes months after the conversation.

Let people know what you do, so they can help you do it!

In the Next Chapter

You now have the knowledge to get deals coming in. Very soon after people get comfortable with that part of the process, their concern turns to "What do I do when the phone rings?" In other words, will they be able to analyze the deals well enough to know the great opportunities from the dirty dogs.

What a coincidence: That's exactly what we cover in the next chapter.

 ### Always Be On the Lookout for Deals

Donald Trump succeeds as a deal maker because nearly everyone who's anyone knows that Donald Trump is open to offers. From his early years, he mastered the art of self-promotion. He not only searches for opportunities but continuously invites opportunities to come to him.

Trump said: "As I was heading in from the Palm Beach airport, a pair of newly built gleaming white towers caught my eye. I looked into who owned them and discovered that a bank had just foreclosed their mortgage. I soon bought the $120 million project for $40 million.

You can find good deals everywhere if you just keep your eyes and your mind open to possibilities."

From *Trump University: Real Estate 101,* John Wiley & Sons, 2006, p.217.

4

How to Read a Deal

The sentence above is not quite accurate. Most amateurs don't have
the problem of too many deals crossing their desks. Instead, they convince themselves never to get into commercial investing, because
they're worried that they won't know what to do when the leads do
start coming in.

That's a good problem to have! Do not let your current status stop
you from revving up your deal-attraction engine, which we covered in
the last chapter.

Also realize this: You will at first not be that great at analyzing
deals. So what? You'll probably let some decent ones go by when you
could have made a nice profit on them. So what? Just be patient and
look for a particularly good deal. If you have followed my advice in the
last chapter, you'll be seeing plenty of leads.

Those leads will give you your *deal legs*, just as sailors must cultivate their *sea legs* and get used to the ocean waves.

Fortunately, this is not a vague and slow process. We're going to walk through several simple calculations that will tell you very quickly whether you have a possible deal, or just a dog.

The vast majority of what you see in the market will be of the canine variety.

In Commercial Real Estate, the 80/20 Rule Is More Like the 90/10 Rule

Ever heard of the *Pareto Principle*? It's also known as the *80/20 Rule*. It means that 80 percent of something is usually caused by 20 percent of something else. In sales, for instance, 80 percent of your sales may come from 20 percent of your clients.

Well, in real estate a similar rule is at work, except it could be called the *90/10 Rule*. Try to spend only 10 percent of your time quickly sorting through 90 percent of the deals that come across your desk, because 90 percent of your potential profits will come from that other 10 percent of deals.

As you get better and better at analyzing, you'll also be building better relationships. Your network will know what types of deals you do and the quality of your in-box will improve. After a while, you'll have people sending you only the deals that make sense.

You Need Only 10 Percent of the Numbers to Sort Out 90 Percent of the Deals

If you were so inclined, you could spend months analyzing only one deal. But something tells me you're much more inclined to make money than crunch numbers—am I right?

Fortunately for us nonaccounting types, you need only a handful of critical-but-easy calculations to determine whether or not a deal is a strong candidate.

Commercial properties usually produce income. There are three types of income:

1. Gross Potential Income
2. Effective Gross Income
3. Net Operating Income

Gross Potential Income is all the money that comes into the property. This includes not only rental income at full occupancy, but vending-machine income, late fees, and anything else collected from the property.

Effective Gross Income is calculated by subtracting the dollar value of vacancies from the gross potential income.

Net Operating Income is the money you have left over after making your mortgage payments and funding capital expenses (for instance, roof repairs). It's usually referred to as *NOI*, and is calculated by subtracting operating expenses from effective gross income.

NOI = Effective Gross Income − Operating Expenses

Note that I mentioned two types of expenses: *Operating Expenses* and *Capital Expenses*. Operating expenses are those that happen during the day-to-day operations of the property. They include taxes, insurance, repairs, maintenance, administrative expenses, management fees, payroll, marketing, contracted services, and utility expenses.

One good feature of operating expenses is that you usually can deduct them from your income taxes in the year in which you paid them.

Capital expenses are typically larger repairs that are not considered immediate. They can only be *depreciated*—that is, deducted—over several years. Examples of capital expenses are replacing roofs, painting the exterior of the property, and replacing appliances and carpet. These are called *below-the-line expenses* because they show up after NOI has been calculated.

We'll come back to these income measurements later.

TOOLS TO CALCULATE VALUE

You need to know two key calculations to determine the value of a property: the *capitalization rate* and the *cash-on-cash return*.

The capitalization rate is usually called the *cap rate*. Think of it as the return you expect to get on your investment if you paid all cash. You calculate the cap rate by dividing the NOI by the sales price. After all, you calculate the yield on a bond, for instance, by taking your annual bond income and dividing it by the value of the bond. Cap rates are similar.

Cap rates usually range from 6 to 12 percent. The higher the cap rate, the riskier the property, just as the higher the bond interest rate, the riskier the bond.

The more stable the property, the lower the cap rate. You would naturally expect a higher return from a riskier property, right?

Riskier properties are ones that need many repairs, are in bad areas, or were built more than 30 years ago.

Institutional investors have been known to pay very low cap rates for properties. As a very rough rule of thumb, we usually find good deals starting at an 8 cap or better.

Here's the nifty thing about cap rates: If I know I need to pay an 8 cap or better for a deal to work for me, then all I need is the NOI. With that number, I can determine what my maximum offer should be for the property.

Let's say I have a shopping center with an NOI of $545,000. I now know two of the three parts of the equation, and any kid can tell you it's possible to find the third number. All I have to do is divide the NOI of $545,000 by the cap rate of 8 and out pops the $6,812,500:

$$\frac{\$545,000 \text{ NOI}}{.08 \text{ Cap Rate}} = \$6,812,500 \text{ Property Value}$$

I cannot pay more than $6,812,500 for that property. Just remember to convert the cap rate of 8 to the decimal of .08, or your calculation will be off by a factor of 100!

Now let's determine value with the *cash-on-cash return*. I like to use this method when I'm buying, and the cap rate approach when I'm selling.

The cash-on-cash return tells us how fast we will get our money back. That's important because you want to get that money plowed back into doing more deals.

Calculate cash-on-cash return this way: Divide annual cash flow by your acquisition costs (that is, down payment and other up-front expenses):

$$\text{Cash on Cash Return} = \frac{\text{NOI} - \text{Debt Service}}{\text{Acquisition Costs}}$$

(Note: NOI – Debt Service is just another name for Annual Cash Flow.)

Good deals usually have a starting cash-on-cash return of 10 percent or more. There are exceptions, and some brokers may tell you it's not possible to get a 10 percent cash-on-cash return in their market. If you hear this, politely thank them and go on to the next broker. This one has just told you that he's not going to give you what you need to be successful.

Now that we have the basic calculations down, we can very quickly look at a deal and determine if we want to take it to the next step.

The next deal in your pipeline comes in and it's a 5 cap. We don't want to pay anything below an 8 cap, so we will probably pass on that deal. Another one comes in with a 7 percent cash-on-cash return. That's not close to the 10 percent threshold, so you should probably pass on that one too. On the other hand, if the person with that property seems really motivated, you might feel like there's room to negotiate a lower price. In that case it would bring both the cap rate and cash-on-cash return higher.

You can see how these two calculations will very quickly handle most of what your deal pipeline delivers.

If the cap rate or cash-on-cash return is above or close to your target numbers, it's worth spending more time to see if this deal could become a live one. You'll need to analyze further to determine whether you should take the deal to the next stage, and you must analyze quickly: Good deals do not stay on the market long.

Another Key Measure: Debt Coverage Ratio

Many investors buy based on speculation. They get into a deal that produces very little cash flow and hope to make all their dough from appreciation.

Yes, such deals can work out. It's even sometimes worth getting into a deal with negative cash flow, where the property doesn't throw off cash, but requires cash. Nevertheless, don't bother with these types of deals when you're starting out. There are simply too many properties that generate positive cash flow for you to get involved with a *nail-biter* of a deal early on.

It's important to gauge the health of your deal by calculating its debt coverage ratio:

$$\text{Debt Coverage Ratio} = \frac{\text{NOI}}{\text{Debt Service}}$$

This ratio tells you how many times your NOI covers your mortgage payment. As a rough guide, lenders like to see a debt coverage ratio of at least 1.2 to 1. For every dollar of mortgage payment you must make, you have $1.20 coming in.

The higher the debt coverage ratio, the safer the deal. If you are in a deal with a debt coverage ratio of 1.1, the seller will either need to come down on price or you'll have to put up a higher down payment to drop that loan amount.

Cash Flow Before Taxes

Notice that we're getting deeper into the analysis, but we're still covering common sense measurements. Here's another such number:

$$
\begin{array}{l}
\text{Income} \\
- \text{ Expenses} \\
\hline
= \text{ Net Operating Income} \\
- \text{ Debt Service} \\
\hline
= \text{ Cash Flow Before Taxes}
\end{array}
$$

That last number is important because it's beginning to approach what we could see in cash flow from the property. We may or may not have much of a tax bill, depending on the deal. Real estate definitely receives favorable tax treatment from Uncle Sam, in the form of depreciation of the property and also deduction of many expenses.

We can't spend that *cash flow before taxes* just yet, but remember that it's the critical number in the calculation we did earlier:

$$
\text{Cash on Cash Return} = \frac{\substack{\text{Cash Flow Before Taxes} \\ \text{(i.e. NOI} - \text{Debt Service)}}}{\text{Acquisition Costs}}
$$

We especially want to know that cash flow figure for two reasons: Not only is it the first benefit we'll receive from the deal, but it's also a measure of our safety cushion.

If a deal generates substantial cash flow, then lots of things can go wrong with the property, but you can still keep current on the bills. Perhaps there are unexpected expenses for repairs or higher-than-normal tenant turnover. Whatever the reason, your cash flow may suffer, but your property won't.

If your deal barely generates cash flow, then what happens when that unforeseen situation occurs? Very quickly, you get into hot water with the lender or with vendors who want to be paid, or both.

Some day your real estate empire will be large enough for you to pay out of your pocket to help a great deal that needs a brief injection of cash. In the meantime, just make sure you go into each deal with a cushion of cash built right in.

THE BIG LIE: PRO FORMA NUMBERS

The term *pro forma* is not Latin for *pretend*, but it might as well be. Most sellers try to give you a work of fiction when they hand over pro forma numbers.

Smart investors always buy based on *actual results*. They focus on numbers that the property is hitting *right now*, and they focus on recent trends. Sellers tend to downplay the past and present, while talking up the future.

It all comes down to a variation on this story line: "Just wait until you see how this property will turn the corner in the near future and become a cash cow."

There are two problems with pro forma numbers: First, if you buy based on them, you're already behind. You must hope that conditions get better simply to meet those projections. But what if the market changes, a hurricane blows in, or a big local employer goes bust? Now things are getting worse, and you bought on the hope that they would get better.

The second problem: You're rewarding the seller for something that she didn't do. She could have raised the rents, increased occupancy, or decreased expenses, but no: She pawned that job off on you—but she wants you to pay her the same as if she had done all these things!

I've bought and sold other businesses. When you buy a business, you should base your decision on the fixed assets and the income stream, not on promises.

The Right Numbers

Here's how the professionals take a quick but accurate look at deals: They focus on the last two years of *profit-and-loss statements*, the year-to-date *profit-and-loss statement*, and the current *rent roll*.

These numbers will tell you the true story of that property.

The profit-and-loss statements are also called *operating statements*. Make sure you get them in the form of a *month-to-month trending report*. It's vital that you see them each month, side-by-side, for an entire year. Then with a glance you can see if the property is flat, trending upward, or losing ground.

This report will also show you how the property performs through the seasons. It's detailed enough that you can drill down and ask questions, but it's not so detailed that you miss the bigger picture.

You want at least the last two years of these statements, although some investors like to get three years. Either way, it's the last six months that you focus on. They're not only the freshest results, but lenders weigh that period very heavily when they're in a loan committee, deciding whether to fund your deal.

Insider Tip

Let's say your deal analysis goes well, and you not only sign a letter of intent to begin your analysis in earnest, but you sign the *purchase and sale agreement*, also known as a *P&S*. That means you'll be buying the property, barring any major unforeseen circumstances.

A couple of months are likely to pass between the time you sign that P&S and the day you actually close on the property. Do not forget to get updated operating statements for those most recent months! Not only will you want the freshest information, but if the numbers are trending down, the lender may require that you put up more money to close the deal. A good closing is one where no such nasty surprises pop up.

The Three Ways to Value Properties

As investors, we benefit by the inexact nature of real estate prices. It's a teachable skill to spot undervalued properties. Part of that skill involves knowing how professionals arrive at fair values for properties. Let's look at the three most common methods.

Comparable Method

This method compares properties that share a similar form and function. For instance, a class-B apartment complex would be compared to a similar class-B property. A 15,000-square-foot retail strip center would be compared to a property of similar size and age.

With commercial properties, you compare not only sales prices but also price-per-square-foot. When comparing apartment complexes, you'll often compare price per unit.

One problem with the comparable method is that your market might not contain other properties that are truly comparable.

Income Method

I said in an earlier chapter that the value of a commercial property is not so much in the property, but in the cash flow it generates. You determine the key cash flow number by taking annual income and subtracting expenses. This is the NOI we've already discussed.

Notice that you do not take into consideration the mortgage amount. That's not a property characteristic because you might buy for all cash and I might buy with lots of debt. Either way, it's the same property.

With the *income approach*, you will use the cap rate to determine the value of the property. Let's look at that formula again:

$$\text{Property Value} = \frac{\text{NOI}}{\text{Cap Rate}}$$

We know the NOI, and I just said we plug in cap rate to determine value. You might wonder what cap rate to use. Here's where we get back to comparables again. This time, instead of trying to compare properties of similar age and size, you find out what the current cap rate is for properties like yours.

Earlier I talked about cultivating real estate brokers to send you leads. These people are also indispensable for valuations. Call up your brokers and ask what the cap rate is for your general type of property. Armed with that information, you can now solve the equation just mentioned for property value.

Let's say you have an industrial building that is bringing in $342,000 in NOI. You talk to a couple of commercial brokers and find out that industrial buildings similar to yours in age and condition are selling at around an 8 cap.

That means:

$$\$4,275,000 = \frac{\$342,000}{.08}$$

Is that THE value of the property? Probably not. But it might be one good estimate.

Cost Method

This is the least-used method. However, it does work well when a property is new or almost new.

When using the cost method, first determine the value of the land. Do that by using the comparable method for similar parcels of land. Then estimate what it would cost to construct the existing building. If the property was built some time ago, you must factor in elements such as obsolescence. Today properties are constructed with more energy efficiency in mind, and they are prewired for lots of technology. Buildings that are only a decade old may not have such features.

This method can still be useful, though. When I started to buy small commercial properties in a worn-out blue-collar city, everyone told me I was crazy. But I didn't care, because I had run two simple calculations—I knew these properties generated good NOI, and I would be buying the properties well below replacement cost.

I scooped up as many of those properties as I could while the market was soft. In a few short years I was rewarded handsomely when my cash flow and values tripled.

Be on the lookout for markets where you can buy buildings below replacement cost. It will discourage builders from coming into that market because—all else being equal—they'll find it hard to compete with you, given their higher price to build.

OTHER IMPORTANT COMPONENTS OF VALUE

Those three methods are just the beginning steps to becoming comfortable with value. Let's look at several other considerations.

Location

You've no doubt heard the old saying that *the three most important things in real estate are location, location, location.* It's a cute saying, but wrong. As with most sayings, it's simplistic. Location is indeed important, but it's only one factor.

You definitely want to spend time assessing the location, though. For instance, most successful coffee and doughnut shops are on the going-into-town side of the road, where most commuters drive in the morning. This is called the A.M. *side.* Most successful dry cleaners are located on the P.M. *side,* going out of town.

You'll see shopping centers off major highways and office buildings near mass-transit lines or major arteries. Hotels often prefer the central business district and airports.

Each commercial property type has its own profile for best location to ensure that it's getting maximum exposure to its target market.

You know those small black hoses stretched across roads for a couple of weeks at a time? Someone's counting traffic. Well-established businesses are very good at knowing what demographics they need to be successful, and an accurate traffic count in front of a commercial building is a key selling point. It's especially important for retail properties, but not as important for industrial, office, or apartment buildings.

Another way to focus on location is to look for up-and-coming areas. If you can get in on the ground floor, you'll make a bundle when the area matures. I encourage you to get my book on the subject, called *Emerging Real Estate Markets*, published by John Wiley & Sons.

When you notice an area where buildings are being rehabbed and new construction is going up, you can bet this area is being revitalized. What was once a poor location may now become desirable.

Just be careful: Enter a *revitalization zone* only after other investors and the local government have committed to the project. Why? Significant change is often very slow to occur. If you start to buy and rehab properties too early, you may be left carrying those properties financially for a long time before your plan comes to fruition.

Don't be a pioneer. You can tell these people because they're the ones face-down in the mud with all the arrows in their backs. Instead, be a fast follower, who doesn't get in quite on the ground floor, but doesn't take nearly the amount of risk, either.

Expenses

Always focus on the expenses your seller is reporting to you. Expenses at most properties run at around 50 percent of gross income, as a general rule. If expenses are running higher, it could indicate inefficient management, or an owner who is paying expenses such as utilities for tenants.

Also look at expenses per square foot. Divide total expenses by the number of rentable square feet. Each area and property type has a normal range. Any broker, property manager, or appraiser on your team can give you this information.

Expenses per unit are calculated by taking the total expenses and dividing them by the total number of units in the property.

Price

When evaluating a multi-family property, find out what the per-unit sales price was for similar properties. You can bet your lender will want to know.

I was initially considering a property in Huntsville, Alabama, for $23,000 per unit. My local banker told me that similar properties were selling for $19,000 per door.

I went right back to the seller and told him that. When he realized I was willing to walk from the deal, the seller came way down on his price. That one conversation with my banker saved me big money.

Be sure to verify taxes with the local assessor's office before you finish your analysis of the property. Assessors have a habit of reevaluating properties at the time of sale and increasing the taxes. I do not like surprises.

If the assessment is more than 40 percent below market price, assume that the taxes will soon go up and factor that into your numbers.

LEASES IN PLACE

When you buy a commercial property, you are actually buying the leases. This is your cash flow, so really focus on the leases in place.

Some aspects of leases are relatively standard, such as the length, or *term*. For instance, multi-family leases are usually written for a term of one year. Sometimes tenants will move into a property without signing a lease. In most states they become a *tenant at will*, which means their tenancy is renewed every 30 days.

Other commercial properties like office buildings usually have leases for three or more years. Some leases—especially on land—can go out as far as 99 years. Why not 100 years? Because real estate law considers any lease over 99 years to be a sale.

You must look at the term of *all* existing leases in a property when doing your due diligence. If the market has risen and rent per square foot is up, you may not be able to take advantage of that rising market if you have leases that expire years from now.

Similarly, watch out if rents are dropping and most leases for major tenants will come due in a year or two. The value of the property will soon fall unless the market changes or you do some fancy negotiating.

The creditworthiness of the tenants or *lessees* is important. With office, retail, and industrial properties, the better their credit, the more steady your cash flow will be. On the other hand, these types of tenants know they have great credit, and will negotiate you down on price. Most things are a tradeoff, and this is no different.

When you continue this lease audit, check to see whether the rent roll the seller gave you in fact matches the sum of individual leases in terms of rents and deposits. If they don't match, you may now have another negotiating point, depending on the magnitude of the discrepancy.

There are an infinite variety of lease clauses. Similar to trusts, they can be written to favor the seller, favor the buyer, or can be pretty neutral. When you get serious about buying or selling any commercial property, be certain you have a highly experienced real estate attorney. This person can alert you to minefields in the leases, and can also get you the most favorable legal treatment possible when the time comes to sign new leases.

Types of Commercial Leases

Be aware of these common forms of commercial leases:

- The *gross lease* is where the owner pays all operating expenses and gets them back by charging higher rents to lessees. These expenses include management fees, common-area maintenance, taxes, insurance, and so on.
- The *modified gross lease* is very similar to the gross lease but certain expenses are passed through to the tenant. These are appropriately called *pass-through expenses*. They usually are taxes, maintenance, insurance, or any combination of these.
- The *net lease* requires tenants to pay operating expenses and common-area maintenance. It's *net* because the landlord is receiving revenue net of all these expenses. A very common form is the *triple-net lease*, where tenants pay all operating

expenses. There are also *single-net leases*, in which tenants pay property taxes and *double-net leases*, where tenants also pay insurance.

Estoppel Letter

This is a letter that's sent to tenants by an independent third party to verify the rents they are actually paying.

The lease may state one amount that is backed up by the rent roll, but these numbers can be altered. Sometimes owners have side deals with tenants that don't show up on the rent roll or leases. These letters will allow you to verify the true income for the property, and this is critical.

To find out exactly what the tenant is paying—and what tenants' actual security deposits are—be sure to have estoppel letters sent. Then check for discrepancies.

Estoppels are used in most commercial transactions, but are very rarely used in multi-family transactions.

Replacement Reserves

Be sure to include replacement reserves in your analysis. Your lender will require that you set aside a certain amount of money in an escrow account for replacement of capital items that wear out over time.

Capital items are larger expenses such as roofs, siding, heating and air-conditioning equipment, parking lot repair, and so on. If you have an A property that was just built, you won't have capital expenses to speak of. With a C property, you can expect significant replacements. Remember that C properties were built 25 to 35 years ago. Unless it's a Japanese shrine that was built for the ages, it's going to need a lot of costly attention.

You *will* get that money back, but only after you spend it. Typically, you can request that reserves be given back to you from the lender every quarter. You must submit all paid invoices to back up your reserve request. You will only get an amount of money that equals your invoices.

Parking

Parking is very important at commercial properties. With office and retail spaces, look for a ratio of four spaces per 1,000 square feet. For an apartment complex, you'll want to see at least 1.5 spaces per unit.

If you're considering converting an apartment complex into condominiums, then you'll want two spaces per unit, because this is the typical ordinance for condos.

I've passed on many otherwise solid deals because the parking was either not adequate or I could not add it cost-effectively.

Breakeven Analysis

Before we run the numbers on a couple of deals, let's first talk about your *breakeven occupancy*. This is a critical calculation, because if your property drops below this mark, your property will not be supporting you; instead, you will be using money to support *it*.

If you have a property whose breakeven occupancy is 82 percent, you must keep it economically occupied at 82 percent to pay expenses and debt service.

Notice that I said *economically occupied*. There are two types of occupancy: physical and economic. Physical occupancy is the obvious version.

Economic occupancy is the percentage of units that are actually paying you. The other units may not be paying you as a result of a few months of free rent that you gave away in order to get tenants, for example. Economic occupancy usually lags physical occupancy by a couple of percentage points and sometimes more, depending on the type of property you encounter.

The higher the breakeven point, the riskier the property.

TYPES OF PROPERTIES

Just like the letter grades you were given in school, commercial properties are rated from *Class A* to *Class D*.

Sellers and brokers classify properties in the same way. *Class A* properties were typically built within the past ten years. They have the trendiest amenities and are crisp and clean. They attract the highest-quality tenants and command the highest lease rates.

Class B properties were built within the past 20 to 30 years. They also attract high-grade tenants, but often the tenants don't quite want to pay for the Class-A space.

Class C properties were built within the last 25 to 35years. These properties are usually in areas with lower-income demographics. They often suffer from deferred maintenance, but there is still a semblance of tenant service.

Class D properties are in the worst condition and are usually in the worst part of town. Buying these properties is a real professional's game. It's possible to make good money by buying D properties in B or A areas and repairing them to B status. This is a form of *repositioning*.

SEEING OPPORTUNITY WHERE OTHERS WALK RIGHT BY

When you invest in commercial properties, you'll have the opportunity to do two types of deals. The first type—which we've been discussing all along—is the *momentum play*. Those are the ones that generate cash flow right from the time of closing. You close on the deal, hand the property to the management company, and start collecting checks.

I suggest that you focus on these lovelies initially, because they provide momentum to your real estate career in the form of check after check.

The other type is a *repositioning deal*. You're repositioning two things—the property itself and the tenant base. The trick is to find a lower-grade property in a better area. It's common to reposition a C property in a B area, and turn it into a B property.

You do this by upgrading the exterior and interior of the complex. Then you reposition the tenant base by getting in a better group of people who are happy to pay B rents for a B property. There is a whole process for doing this, and I outline it in my book, *Multi-Family Millions*, published by John Wiley & Sons (2008).

I'm not talking about slapping a new coat of paint on a property and charging more. If you reposition incorrectly, you simply pour money down the drain. If you do it properly, and give the right time and attention to each phase, it can be wildly profitable.

The ultimate is to reposition a property in an emerging market, where not only the property and tenants get better, but the entire market takes off. You only need to do one of these deals in your lifetime to put a permanent grin on your face and lots of zeros on your bank balance.

How to Run the Numbers

Let's sink our teeth into a couple of deals and see how the analysis works.

Have the past two years' operating statements broken down into a twelve-month trend report showing each month side by side. You'll also need the year-to-date operating statements broken down the same way, plus the current rent roll. Remember, we don't care about the seller's projections or *pro forma* numbers. We don't want the thrilling fiction the seller hands us about future performance, but instead want to focus on the nonfiction of past and present results.

Note: Occasionally a seller will not give you actual numbers until you put in an offer. This is crazy because you can't make a rational offer without them.

If this happens, consider moving on to the next deal. If you really want to pursue this one, the only thing you can do is offer based on the numbers you were given. Then, once you get the actual numbers, you can renegotiate your offer if those numbers are drastically different.

Case Study 1: Apartment Complex

You get a property package for a 144-unit apartment complex. It was built in 1984 and tenants pay all the utilities. The seller is asking a purchase price of $5.4 million. Assume that you will take out an interest-only loan at 6 percent, and you and your partners are putting 20 percent down on the deal. (Remember, that doesn't mean *you* are putting anything down. That's the beauty of having partners who are private lenders.)

The seller tells you that gross potential rent is $972,000 per year and you determine the vacancy rate is 8 percent.

You don't care what the theoretical revenue is, because vacancies exist at the property. Therefore, you want to get to the effective gross income:

Effective Gross Income = Gross Potential Rent − Vacancy Cost

First calculate the vacancy cost:

$77,760 Vacancy Cost = $972,000 × .08 Vacancy

Now calculate Effective Gross Income, or *EGI*:

894,240 EGI = $972,000 Gross Potential Rent − $77,760 Vacancy Cost

The seller also gives you the following actual expenses, which add up to Total Operating Expenses:

Taxes	$67,200
Insurance	$36,000
Labor	$129,600
Administrative	$15,800
Utilities	$48,000
Repairs and Maintenance	$115,200
Marketing	$10,800
Capital Reserves	$36,000
Total Operating Expenses	$458,600

Now let's find the net operating income:

NOI = Effective Gross Income − Total Operating Costs

Putting numbers to this equation, we find:

435,640 NOI = 894,240 − 458,600

Now that we know the NOI, we can determine the capitalization rate:

$$\text{Capitalization Rate} = \frac{\text{NOI}}{\text{Sales Price}}$$

Our situation, with numbers filled in, is:

$$.08 = \frac{\$435,640}{\$5,400,000}$$

We now know the capitalization rate is 8 (remember to bring the decimal point over two places).

Now let's figure the cash-on-cash return, which you saw earlier:

$$\text{Cash-on-Cash Return} = \frac{\text{NOI} - \text{Debt Service}}{\text{Acquisition Costs}}$$

We know the NOI, and we now determine debt service and acquisition costs.

We are putting 20 percent down, so the mortgage will be 80 percent of the purchase price:

$4,320,000 Mortgage = $5,400,000 Purchase Price × .80

With an interest-only mortgage at 6 percent, our annual debt service would be:

$259,000 Annual Debt Service = .06 × $4,320,000 Mortgage

Your acquisition costs will be the down payment, plus any out-of-pocket cost needed to close the deal. The down payment for this deal is 20 percent:

$1,080,000 Down Payment = .20 × $5,400,000 Purchase Price

Out-of-pocket costs typically run at 3 percent of the purchase price:

$162,000 Out-of-Pocket Cost = .03 × $5,400,000 Purchase Price

Therefore:

$1,242,000 Total
Acquisition Costs = $1,080,000 Down Payment +
$162,000 Out-of-Pocket Costs

We now can plug everything in for an answer:

$$.14 \text{ Cash-on-Cash Return} = \frac{\$435,640 \text{ NOI} - \$259,000 \text{ Debt Service}}{\$1,242,000 \text{ Acquisition Costs}}$$

A 14 percent cash-on-cash return is good. As I said, you usually want 10 percent or better. This deal is worth pursuing.

Case Study 2: Shopping Center

Another broker calls you with a heads-up that a shopping center has just come on the market this morning. It is 45,000 square feet and is anchored by a major-chain grocery store. (An *anchor* is the largest tenant.) There are six other retail stores in the complex. The square footage and rent breakdown is as follows:

Leases	Sq. Ft.	Rent per Sq. Ft.	Yearly Rent
Grocery store	11,000	$12	$132,000
Pharmacy	8,000	$11	$88,000
Shoe store	5,000	$8	$40,000
Nutrition store	2,000	$6	$12,000
Clothing store	8,000	$8	$64,000
Electronics store	7,000	$7	$49,000
Hair salon	2,000	$6	$12,000
Pizza parlor	2,000	$6	$12,000
Total	**45,000**		**$409,000**

All leases are *triple-net*, with tenants also paying the *common-area maintenance expenses*, or *CAM*, of $3,500 per month.

The purchase price is $5 million. You and your partners would put 20 percent down and take out an interest-only loan at 6.5 percent.

We already know the NOI for this property is $409,000, because tenants pay expenses under the triple-net leases, and the owner bills back the CAM expenses. We also know that:

$$\text{Capitalization Rate} = \text{NOI/Purchase Price}$$

$$.081 \text{ Cap Rate} = \frac{\$409,000 \; NOI}{\$5,000,000 \; \text{Purchase Price}}$$

In other words, it is an 8.1 cap rate.

Now let's determine the Cash-on- Cash Return:

$$\text{Cash-on-Cash Return} = \frac{\text{NOI} - \text{Debt Service}}{\text{Acquisition Costs}}$$

$$\$4,000,000 \text{ Mortgage Amount} = \$5,000,000 \text{ Purchase Price} \times .80 \text{ Financing}$$

Now let's find the annual payment on that mortgage:

$$\$260,000 \text{ Debt Service} = \$4,000,000 \text{ Mortgage Amount} \times .065 \text{ Interest Rate}$$

Now let's figure acquisition costs:

$$\$1,000,000 \text{ Down Payment} = .20 \times \$5,000,000 \text{ Purchase Price}$$

$$\$150,000 \text{ Out-of-Pocket Cost} = .03 \times \$5,000,000 \text{ Purchase Price}$$

Plugging in all our numbers, we get:

$$.129 \text{ Cash-on-Cash Return} = \frac{\$409,000 \; NOI - \$260,000 \text{ Debt Service}}{\$1,150,000 \text{ Acquisition Costs}}$$

In other words, a 12.9 percent cash-on-cash return, which is not bad.

Am I saying that this quick analysis is enough to buy a property? Of course not. But it is enough to do that quick, initial review of all the deals that will soon be coming into your life.

Remember, you will apply the *90/10 Rule* and spend only 10 percent of your time on 90 percent of the deals. That will allow you and your team to focus the bulk of your efforts on only the most promising deals.

How to Borrow an Additional Set of Eyes

Let's say that you review a deal and get pretty excited. Start the offer process immediately, and send that deal to your mortgage broker to have him take a look at the numbers.

It's critical that you have a good mortgage broker on your team. If this person is well-connected, he knows which lenders specialize in what types of loans.

This service alone is worth the *one point* (that is, one percent of the loan amount) that you'll pay the broker for putting the financing together.

If you try to save money here, you will waste a lot of time looking for the right lender for your deal. Not only will you often be rejected, but—and this can be worse—you may get a *false yes*. What I mean by this is that a lender will tell you that it can do the deal, but it really cannot. This can be disastrous.

This happened to me on a large repositioning deal. I went with a lender who said it could do the construction loan, and when construction was complete, the lender would roll it over to a conventional loan.

Six weeks into the process the lender called to say it didn't want to do the deal. That really got my attention. I was now looking at eating a lot of expenses if I had to back out of the deal, not to mention the damage to my reputation.

Fortunately, I had a great relationship with the bank that currently held the note on that property, and I arranged for alternate financing.

I later talked about this fiasco with an experienced local mortgage broker who smiled, nodded, and said that he could have told me that the lender had a reputation for not following through with that type of deal! I've been glad to pay experienced mortgage brokers for their invaluable knowledge ever since.

Brokers not only save you time and trouble with lenders, but they double-check your analysis and make sure you got it right. It's like having an expert deal analyst on your team.

After you do your first deal, you'll have many brokers and sellers sending you deals. If you cultivate your mortgage broker correctly, you can even have this person do the preliminary screening of the deals. Imagine only hearing about a deal when your broker says that it's a live prospect, and that he already has a lender in mind. That is the true power of your team.

In the Next Chapter

You don't have to be Donald Trump in order to be an excellent negotiator. You'll find that most people you'll be sitting across the table from are poor negotiators. Therefore, with only a few solid principles under your belt, you'll do a great job of buying for the least money and selling for the most.

In the next chapter I hand you a career's worth of profitable negotiating principles.

5

LOCKING IN YOUR PROFIT

THE LETTER OF INTENT

You have discovered how to attract deals and create key relationships. You also know how to leverage your time and quickly find the nuggets among all the ore you're sifting through. It's time to start making offers on the deals that make sense.

When we make an offer on a commercial deal, we use what's called a *Letter of Intent*. It's also known as the *LOI*. This short document tells the seller the terms under which you wish to purchase the deal.

Many beginning investors make a big mistake right here. They think the purpose of doing due diligence is to end up making an offer. In reality, the purpose of making an offer is to allow you the time and access to information in order to perform effective due diligence.

When a broker approaches you on a deal, you have only the roughest numbers, as we saw in the last chapter. Now it's time to get more serious about the deal. There's no point sinking lots of your time into a deal, only to find out it was sold last week to someone else. The LOI enables you and the seller to date seriously, so to speak, before you sign the *Purchase and Sale Agreement* and get engaged.

The LOI covers several key aspects of the deal. These include:

- Property address
- Purchase price
- Time frame
- Inspection period
- Deposit
- Title policy
- Closing
- Assignment
- Access
- Commissions

Let's look at each of these in more detail.

Property Address

Do not refer to the property only by its business name, such as Evergreen Mall. Be sure to use the address of the property so that there is no confusion at any stage with similarly named properties.

Purchase Price

This is what you are willing to pay for the property, plus any other requests regarding the price of the property. For instance, I usually add a *repair allowance* in this section.

A repair allowance is what you will receive from the seller at closing for repairs that must be done to the property. Most properties need immediate repairs at the time of sale. Some properties need much more than others. I would rather get those repair dollars from the seller instead of having to go into my own pocket to finance them.

If the seller does not want to give a repair allowance, ask him to raise the price by the amount of the repair allowance and then give that amount to you at closing. He should be agreeable, because these costs are a deductible expense to him at the closing and he won't pay taxes on that extra money. Most sellers are willing to do this.

Just be certain of two things: The property appraisal must support these extra dollars for repair; otherwise, why are you buying it? Second, you'll need to redo your numbers and make sure you still make a profit at the higher purchase price.

Some sellers offer to lower the purchase price by the amount of the repair allowance and have you pay for the repairs. Again, this means you must finance those repairs somehow, and that can be a pain. It's better to have the repair allowance built right into the deal.

The *purchase price* section of the LOI is also where you ask the seller to hold any owner financing. Some sellers own properties free and clear of any debt. If you never ask for seller financing, you're unlikely to get it! Some sellers will give you much or all of the financing you need for the deal. You can't count on it, but it's worth asking.

Most likely you will be asking for a second mortgage of between 10 and 20 percent. First you must find out if your primary lender will even allow a second mortgage, in the form of seller financing. Some will, and others won't. Such a loan is called *subordinated debt*. If you truly need it to make the numbers work, tell your mortgage broker to find a lender who will allow it.

When you prepare your LOI including a proposal for owner financing, be sure to start the offer process in a way that benefits you the most.

The first offer I always make is for the *principal to be paid in five years*. Notice that I didn't say anything about interest or payments. What I'm asking for is a five-year loan to be paid off in five years in one lump sum.

Why would someone give me a loan for five years and not want to see any money sooner in the form of principal or interest payments? I don't always know why people do that, but I know it happens. Why not start your LOI negotiations by asking for it?

If that goes nowhere, my second seller-financing request is for a loan with *simple interest at x percent to be paid in five years*. In other words, if the seller insists on getting interest, offer simple interest to be paid with the principal in five years. This again avoids making payments. Cash flow is king in our business; you must guard it energetically.

If the seller balks at that request, at least he knows you're negotiating like a pro! Your third offer will be for *simple interest payments monthly, principal to be paid in five years*. Save this version for when the seller insists on a monthly payment.

Your fourth negotiating position is reserved for the moment when the seller insists on acting like a bank and getting principal and interest payments monthly. Your offer then might be *10 percent owner-financing amortized over 25 years, with a 5-year balloon*.

Translated, that means the loan payments will be calculated as though you will pay them over 25 years, and for the first five years of payments, that's all you will pay. However, at the end of five years, you'll make one large payment to bring the loan up to fully-paid status. This has the effect of dropping five years of your payments to a lower level.

I know this sounds like a lot of back-and-forth with the seller. Believe me, it's worth it. Besides, some sellers will accept your very first offer.

Time Frame

A typical timeframe clause looks like this:

> Seller shall submit a *bona fide* Purchase and Sale Agreement (the "Agreement") to Buyer with respect to the purchase and sale of the Property within ten (10) business days from the date this letter of intent is fully executed and accepted by both parties. The date the Agreement is executed by both Buyer and Seller and receipted with the Title Company (as hereinafter defined) shall be the Effective Date of the Agreement. Buyer shall have Thirty (30) days after Effective Date (the "Inspection Period") to make best efforts to perform physical inspections and other due diligence with respect to the Property and decide, in Buyer's sole discretion, whether the Property is satisfactory to Buyer.

The *Effective Date* mentioned above is very important. It's the date on which both the seller and buyer are agreeing to sign the purchase and sale agreement.

Every other important date in the contract will be based on that Effective Date.

Inspection Period

As you can see from the earlier paragraph, the *Inspection Period* lasts for 30 days after the Effective Date. This is also called the *Due Diligence Period*.

This is when you really roll up your sleeves and have a detailed look at the property. It's when you do three major inspections— financial, physical, and legal (we cover this in a later chapter). During the Inspection Period, if you are not satisfied with the property for any reason, you can walk away and get back your entire deposit.

It's vital that you remain constantly aware of your Effective Date: Should you decide to walk away from the deal after that date passes, you will get none of your money back.

Your due diligence information request from the seller will include:

- Current title commitment paid for by seller
- Any property survey the seller has
- Existing leases, current rent roll (showing lease rent, lease expiration, and security deposits paid for every tenant)
- Bank deposits for the most recent three months (certified by the bank)
- Profit-and-loss statements for the past three years
- Capital expenditures for the past three years
- Architectural, engineering, and feasibility studies as to the condition of the property, if the owner has these documents
- Environmental reports (Phase I or other reports), if these are in the owner's possession
- Inventory of personal property used in connection with the property
- Real estate tax and insurance bills for the previous two years
- All active service agreements with vendors

You may very well be told that some of this information is not available, as in "I have two years of profit-and-loss statements, but not for the third year." This is not a reason to kill the deal right away, because you may be able to get the information in other ways. For instance, the profit-and-loss might be reconstructed through inspecting vendor invoices and utility bills.

It comes down to just how good the deal is: If it looks really good, you won't mind working harder for the information. If it's a so-so deal, you may be right in dropping the offer and moving on to the greener pastures that your marketing machine will soon direct you to.

Attach this *laundry list* to your LOI, but don't sweat the details: I explain all of these items and the entire due diligence process in the next chapter.

Deposit

You'll usually put between one and three percent of the purchase price down as a deposit. (This money will be held in escrow until the closing and will be credited to you at the closing.) You will get this money back if you walk away from the deal within the Inspection Period—that is, as long as you didn't offer *hard money* at the time of deposit.

Hard money means you agree that you won't get that money back if you decide to drop out of the deal. Why would you ever offer such a thing? Some sellers require that you put up hard money at the beginning of a deal.

I don't recommend this. If you do, you had better be sure that you've done a lot of your homework before you get into the deal, and that it has a very high probability of going through. As with most things, it's a judgment call relating to just how good the deal is. Resist the temptation until you get extremely comfortable analyzing deals, and even then put down hard money very sparingly.

Your deposit automatically turns into hard money after the inspection period is up. Sometimes a seller will require a second deposit after the inspection period, and this money will immediately *go hard*.

Title Policy

Include an item in your LOI that states: "Seller shall convey good and merchantable title to the property to Buyer." This is of course assumed, but you still want it explicitly stipulated in your offer. Here's another tip: Make the title work a seller expense. Lately, I've seen sellers trying to push this cost off onto buyers. Don't let it become a *deal breaker*, but try to have the seller pay for it.

Closing

This paragraph spells out exactly when you plan on closing on the property. It is usually a certain number of days after the effective date or after the inspection period.

Typical closings happen between 60 and 90 days after the effective date, or 30 to 45 days after the inspection period has ended.

Assignment

Add a paragraph that allows you to assign the contract to a third party. This means you can flip a property quickly without first going through a closing. You can also use this clause to move your property from one entity to another.

In most cases, I'll take a property under contract using my company name, The Lindahl Group, LLC. Then I transfer it to the entity that will ultimately hold the property during the period I own it. I'll name that entity *[property name], LLC*. For instance, if it's the Cherry Creek Mall, I'll name it *Cherry Creek, LLC*. (I don't want to spend the money on setting up an LLC until I know that the deal will go through.)

There's no need to get cute with the names. There is a mistaken notion that different names will throw off attorneys who are trying to find your properties. The name won't slow down anyone but you, as you continually try to remember whether Acme LLC is your Cherry Creek property in Denver or the Pheasant Run property in Raleigh.

Access

Your LOI must state that you and any third-party contractor whom you bring to the site (roofer, inspector, and so on) will have reasonable access to the property during the inspection period.

You must give *reasonable notice* before you show up each time. A 48-hour notice is considered reasonable.

Commissions

Just so everyone is on the same page, state clearly who pays which commissions. Usually the seller pays the real estate broker's commission, unless you are using a buyer's broker.

HERE'S WHERE YOU ROLL UP YOUR SLEEVES

Now that you know how to put together an LOI, it's time to go through the negotiating process so that you have the joy of possessing a LOI that's signed by both parties. It's the only kind that counts.

You can actually put your own signature on the LOI before or after you negotiate. (Remember: You can withdraw it during the inspection period and get your money back if something goes wrong.) If you're dealing with a broker, you may send over a signed LOI to start the negotiations. If you're dealing directly with an owner, you might meet with the owner, negotiate the terms, and then draw up the LOI.

Regardless of how you do it, don't commit the same mistake I did many years ago. (You'll see it on the next page.)

HOW TO PRESENT YOUR OFFER DIRECTLY TO A SELLER

When possible, I like to negotiate directly with the seller and with no *middlemen*. This way you can feel the pulse of the negotiations and change strategies in midstream if you have to.

AMATEUR MISTAKE: "HONEST PEOPLE GIVE THEIR BEST OFFER UP FRONT."

When I started to negotiate my deals, the seller or broker would ask me how much I would like to offer on the property. Like a dummy, I would tell her my real number.

Why is that dumb? Because naturally the broker or seller would counter with a higher price. I'd be immediately forced into one of two bad alternatives: Either I could violate my own best offer, or I could say "My offer is final."

Now what room did I just give the seller to negotiate? I'm making the seller look bad by insisting that the only party to be flexible on price is the other person.

I lost a few deals before I realized that it's not a matter of honesty, but of negotiating manners. People want to feel good about how the negotiation turns out. They frequently come into a negotiation feeling that the other side is better prepared, or in some way has the upper hand.

When you position yourself so that you can come down on price, or throw something else into the deal to sweeten it, you enhance that person's self-esteem instead of squashing it.

If you're not already convinced, think how you would feel if the next time you made your first offer for something expensive, the other person grinned broadly and said "Yes sir! No problem!"

You would instantly feel that you were being taken advantage of, because the other person is so happy. It would make you wonder how much money you had just left on the table. If, instead, you had to go a couple of rounds with the other party, and each side somewhat reluctantly agreed to a middle price, you would feel better. When your boss or spouse asks "How did it go," you would be able to say "Well, I went up on price, but he had to come down, too."

One time I put an offer on a property in Montgomery, Alabama. The owner was asking $2.2 million. I did my numbers and the property *penciled-out* at that; in other words, it was worth that price. I offered $2.2 million, thinking, "Great, we have a deal."

The seller came back with $2.4 million! I had never heard of such a thing before. He had just experienced the feeling that I was taking advantage of him, when I gave in too quickly.

(Continued)

AMATEUR MISTAKE (CONTINUED)

That experience taught me something else: If I do want to offer full price in a competitive situation where there are other bidders, I should throw in some other condition that the seller can say "no" to.

For instance, I should have offered $2.2 million, but requested that the seller take back a second mortgage at ten percent. I didn't need the second mortgage but it would allow the seller to say "no." I'd cave in, and we'd be set at $2.2 million.

I could instead have requested that the seller pay $40,000 in closing costs, or that furniture be left behind. Always be prepared with a couple of these *add-ons*.

Typically, you should start your negotiations at ten percent below your *strike price*. That's the maximum price you will pay for the property.

Oh, and if a broker asks "What's your strike price?" tell him it's none of his business, but say it with a smile! Hold your cards close to your chest.

The best place to negotiate is in *your office*. That will give you the advantage. The worst place is the seller's home or office because that person will have the advantage.

If they won't meet at your place of business—or if you're working out of your basement—then at least meet in a neutral location. A coffee shop, restaurant, or at the property itself are all acceptable locations.

Always look to collect small advantages when you negotiate. Here are a couple:

Sit with your back to the window when you can. This sometimes makes it harder for the person to watch your body language closely; it also can give you a halo effect.

Sit at a rounded table and sit at 90 degrees to each other instead of on opposite sides of the table.

Have everything you will use during your negotiations *on the table when you start*. Do not introduce anything new during the process, or it can confuse the other party and take away any momentum you've built.

When I say *everything*, I mean take out everything: calculator, files, presentation kit, the pen that the seller will use to sign—take it all out.

I discovered this last point the hard way. I was negotiating a deal with a seller at the seller's property. We had been in his office negotiating the price and terms for almost 90 minutes. I finally got him to agree to a price that we both could benefit from.

I then reached behind my back and pulled the LOI folder from my briefcase and merely plopped it on the table. As soon as I did this, I saw the seller move back from the table as if being pushed by some unseen force.

It had taken me 90 minutes for him to finally get comfortable with me and agree to the deal. I blew it because I introduced something that he wasn't comfortable with. It must have looked as though I was concealing something from him. I didn't get anything signed that day.

Questions to Ask

Sometimes a few key questions can really help your negotiations:

"What is it that you're hoping I can do for you?"

By asking this, you're actually asking the seller how he would like to be sold. You want to know how you can make this a win/win situation for both of you. This should be one of the first questions you ask.

After you ask this question and get an answer, then ask:

"Mr. Seller, if I can do that for you, would you be ready to okay the agreement today?"

Never ask the seller to *sign* anything, and don't call the agreement a *contract*. These are spooky words to lots of people, who will freeze and think it over yet again. It's always much better to say "okay the agreement."

"In the past, what have you done to sell your buildings? What worked for you?"

You're again asking the seller to tell you how she would like to be sold. Follow up this question by creating a deal that meets the conditions in her answer.

"What do you plan to do if the building doesn't sell?"

You're implanting a sense of anxiety in the seller if she really needs or wants to sell. It may also indicate to you that the seller is unmotivated if the response is "Oh, I'm fine with holding onto it for a couple more years."

"When did you want to close?"

This helps you to gauge the seller's sense of urgency. Some sellers will be cagey here, but others will come right out and tell you that they're doing a Section 1031 like-kind exchange and they have another 42 days to get it done. You won't know unless you ask. When you do ask, watch the body language closely for signs that confirm or counter her words.

Regardless of what she says, structure your offer around her answer.

"Why do you think it hasn't sold yet?"

This shifts the seller's perspective to one that can help you. It may not only create a little anxiety, but the seller may come right out and tell you what other prospective buyers have said about the property.

"Have you thought about carrying back financing?"

Now you're fishing to see if the seller is willing to take back a mortgage. For every bunch of "No" answers, you'll regularly be surprised by the number of sellers who say, "I'm open to that; what did you have in mind?"

"What will you do with your proceeds?"

This gets your seller's *greed glands* going. Let her tell you what she plans to do with the money. She's spending it in her mind. Keep the conversation going casually about how good that sounds, to be able to move onto that next property, or take that long-awaited cruise. The longer you can get the seller to envision what she plans on doing with the money, the closer you will get to having a signed contract.

Also try to get a series of "yes" answers whenever you can. This is a well-known conditioning process that some highly sophisticated sales organizations use. Getting a series of small "yes" agreements can help you get the big "yes" at the end of your negotiating session.

EVEN MORE NEGOTIATING TIPS

Before we talk about how to present an offer through a real estate broker, here are ten more tips to becoming an effective negotiator:

Discover everything you can about the situation, the issues, and the participants. This is another way of saying *come prepared*. There is no excuse for being unprepared for a negotiating session. The person who is the best prepared usually wins.

Keep on the lookout for what's motivating the seller. Sometimes all you have to do is ask, as I mentioned before. Occasionally you don't even need to do that, because the other person will let slip clues to his motivations. It might be the repetition of a certain comment, or how that person's body language and voice changes when you're talking closing date, but not when you mention price. It's a skill that you'll keep developing over a very long time, but the payoff can happen quickly, so start now.

Set goals. Know what you want to accomplish at each negotiating session. I don't mean generalities such as "Seller signs offer." At what specific price and terms will you be satisfied? Also try to have more than one black-and-white desired outcome. If you can't achieve your ideal result, know what your fallback position will be.

Anticipate the other party's comments and prepare your response. If the seller says your price is too low, what will you say? If the seller wants you to *go hard* with a deposit, what will be your response? What if the seller wants an unreasonably short closing period? These are all situations you should be prepared for.

You won't be able to anticipate all of them, of course. But you should never be caught surprised twice. Become a great note taker after negotiations, writing down the answers to questions such as "What did I learn that can help me in my next negotiation?"

Remain pleasant and unflappable. We're in a numbers game. The investor who cares least almost always wins. If you are doing your marketing properly, you'll have other deals not far behind, so don't wrap your existence up in winning this one.

Build trust. People trust people who listen to them. Repeat or paraphrase what the seller says after she says it. I don't mean parroting back her words, but instead acknowledging the point she is making and building upon it, rather than simply letting it float by while you're busy making your own statements.

Create win/win situations. This is especially important when it looks as though you're at an impasse. By looking for creative ways to build bridges and not walls, you might slowly put that deal together. Not only will the other party see that you're trying, but that person may get in the same creative spirit.

Use empathetic comments and sympathetic gestures to smooth over difficult situations. As I said earlier, people don't care what you know until they know that you care. Sometimes all you need to do is use the other person's name and occasionally smile to inject a different atmosphere into the negotiation. Watch yourself to make sure you pause to consider the other person's statements, and don't just steamroller over them.

Figuratively speaking, try to get on the same side of the table as the other person, and position it as more of a problem-solving task than a win/lose negotiation.

Always underpromise and overdeliver. Remember what I said in an earlier chapter about being easy to do business with? It applies to cultivating your deal-attraction machine, and it certainly applies to negotiating. Be sure to arrive on time. Check that you did all the tasks you were supposed to do after the last meeting. Deliver paperwork and checks earlier than expected. These are all courteous and common sense practices that are extremely rare to find and are highly valued.

How to Present Your Offer to a Real Estate Broker

Sometimes you have to go through a broker in order to negotiate. Whenever possible, see if you can be there when the broker presents your offer to the seller. It gives you a chance to meet with the seller and talk over any issues that may be brewing.

Brokers usually won't allow you to be there, because they think you'll screw up the negotiations. I also own a real estate brokerage company, and I train my agents not to let buyers in the room when the offer is being presented. Still, it's worth asking.

When I tell investors that I'm also a broker, I often get the question, "Do you make your offer from your company to save half the commission?"

The answer is "no," for two reasons. First, because I buy all around the country, I would have to apply for a brokerage license in many states, and it's just not worth the bother.

The second reason is the one you should focus on: I want the seller's broker to get the full commission because if he has another offer pending and it's one of his buyers, he's going to want me to win, even if the other buyer's offer is less than mine.

Let me explain. A broker brings two offers to the seller. One is his own buyer and the second is from another broker—it could be your broker.

This is what the broker is likely to say:

> **Mr. Seller, I'm happy to present two offers to you. One is from a buyer with whom I've worked in the past. She has a solid reputation, her financials are in order, and she is a proven closer. The other offer is from another agent in town. I haven't done much business with him so I'm not sure how he conducts business. I'm not familiar with her buyer, either, but their offer is a little higher.**
>
> **It's up to you—You could go with the proven closer, or you could get a little more money by going with this other buyer . . . I'm just not so sure that we're going to get to the closing table as quickly.**

Do you see what is happening? In my opinion, that's the way it should be. The broker has to feed his family and help grow the company. He really doesn't know anything about the other buyer except what the other broker is telling him. Who knows if that is true or not?

I never *go cheap* and try to get the co-broker commission. Remember, we're trying to create long-term relationships. With that in mind, not only should you not focus on saving a buck, but you should look for ways to pay other people for their efforts and have them want to do business with you.

This brings up another point: Whenever possible, put in your offer through the listing broker. For the exact same reasons that I said not to co-broker, you want your offer presented by the listing broker so that he gets both sides of the commission. You will get more deals if you do this.

When presenting a deal through a broker, see if you can get some price guidance. Ask how much information he is willing to share with you about the seller's motivation, where the seller needs to be on price, and what terms if any the seller is willing to accept.

If you're going through the listing broker, she is more apt to give you some guidance to get that deal done.

Want another tip? When going through the broker, negotiate with that person as if he were the seller. Ask the same questions and also ask the broker to present the offer with the same reasons you just laid out. It respects the broker's status, and helps you win deals in another way:

Sometimes brokers find it helpful when you lay out your arguments to them. They can then use what you tell them with sellers. Of course, you cannot guarantee that they will do this, and you're at their mercy. But when you make their job easier by providing ready-made reasons, you're more likely to have them repeat that reasoning with sellers.

PROVEN METHODS TO INCREASE THE CHANCES
OF GETTING YOUR OFFER ACCEPTED

Build Rapport

This is the very first thing you should do with a seller. People like people who are like them. Search for common ground that you may have with the seller. Do the same with brokers if you're dealing through them.

When talking with a seller, listen to his voice. Does it have a familiar accent? Is he wearing an article of clothing you can quickly compliment?

If you're at a seller's home or business, look around. What do you see that you can relate to? Even if you're just meeting at a restaurant, try to start with small talk about the weather, sports, or noncontroversial news. You may get little or no response, but you're gently fishing. Eventually you will come across a topic that you both find interesting.

Within reason, the more you genuinely talk about that topic, the more the other person will like you and want to do business with you. I'm not suggesting that you become coldly manipulative. Instead, I'm saying that being *all business* is also usually a mistake. Don't ramble on, but do grease the conversation with some nonbusiness human element. It's all part of my rule about being easy to do business with.

The Silent Treatment

Silence makes most people uncomfortable. After you have made an important point, look directly at the other party, smile, and shut up. The longer you go without saying anything, the more uneasy the other person will tend to become. Eventually he will say something—anything—just to break the silence. The response will often be unguarded and give you valuable information.

Over years of negotiating, I've become a big believer in the old saying, "He who speaks first, loses."

The Flinch

I'm talking about a small sound or facial expression that communicates the reflex of displeasure. Imagine that someone told you about a bad fall that some skateboarder took. What kind of a face would you make? That's the kind of face you want to make when you flinch, except more subtly.

When a flinch is done right—meaning subtle but instantaneous—it can plant serious doubts in the other person's mind. Try flinching in reaction to a monetary offer or when the other party starts the negotiations too aggressively. Don't be surprised if even the most experienced negotiator becomes more flexible, without your even saying a word.

The Deadline

Deadlines keep situations under control and deliver results. Begin a meeting by saying you must leave in an hour. Then, when the discussion starts to wander off-track, move things along by reminding them that you must leave soon.

You can sometimes motivate people to take immediate action even if you simply remind them about deadlines, such as the date when your offer will expire.

I strongly recommend that you do not let your offer hang out there too long. If you are making an offer on a smaller commercial property, make it good for 24 hours. When dealing with larger properties, my standard deadline is three days.

The further out you date your offer, the more likely your seller is to *shop it* to other buyers and use your offer to get a better price.

The Japanese are famous for using deadlines to their advantage. When negotiating with foreigners who fly in to negotiate a deal, some Japanese businessmen find out when the other person's flight is scheduled to depart. They then wine-and-dine the other party and treat him like a king for days—right up until a couple of hours before his flight is leaving. This puts a lot of stress on the foreigner not to return home empty-handed. Very shrewd.

The Competition

Mentioning the competition is a good way to keep the other side from feeling too secure. Let him know that you're looking at other properties and expect to have a deal by a certain date. Don't lie, but don't miss the opportunity to use other properties to your advantage.

I like to use this tactic when I'm at an impasse with a seller. I usually say, "Mr. Seller, I *will* buy a property similar to yours within the next 60 days. I have two other potential properties that I'm in negotiations with. Of the three, I'd really like to buy your property, but the choice is yours." I don't pull out this tactic frequently, but I've had good results whenever I've used it.

The Walk-Away Close

Being prepared to walk away from the negotiation can get dramatic results when the other party is being noncommittal or refusing to make a counteroffer. If the negotiation has reached a stalemate, simply start to gather your papers and pack your briefcase in a matter-of-fact manner. If you have read the situation correctly, the other party should offer a constructive response.

If the other party in fact allows you to walk away, make sure you *walk away*! If you don't, you will have blown all of your credibility.

A friend of mine did this masterfully in a very high-pressure situation on Wall Street. When he left, he just made sure to pace himself as he walked to the elevator. Then he slowly pushed the button and got in. He rode the elevator down 35 flights, thinking he had really blown it. As he was slowly walking out the building, a guy came sprinting out of the stairwell to catch up to him, asking him to reconsider! My friend got the deal he was after.

Agree/Repeat

Here is a very powerful pattern you can use in your negotiations. It has four steps and incorporates some of what we've already discussed:

Step 1: Agree/Repeat. When you're talking with a seller, nod or otherwise show agreement with what she says and repeat it in a natural fashion. That shows you are listening. For example, the seller says: "I must get $1 million for my property." You say, "Okay, I understand that you must get $1 million for your property."

Step 2: Answer. Respond to the seller's point. You may need to respond "In my review of the profit-and-loss statements, I see that the property at an 8 cap rate is valued closer to $940,000."

Step 3: Ask a Closing Question. You then ask: "If I could show you a way that I could pay $960,000 but also provide you with a tax shelter and a monthly annuity, could we move ahead to start the paperwork?" Now you *shut up and wait for the seller's response, because* . . .

Step 4: He Who Speaks First, Loses. There is a pause, and finally the seller asks, "How would that work?"

You've just scored a negotiating victory. You're one step closer to scoring the deal.

In case you're wondering: The tax shelter and monthly annuity would come from the second mortgage. The seller would not be taxed on the mortgage amount until he receives the money, and the annuity would come in the form of mortgage payments each month.

Small Moves

This is a splendid negotiating tactic. You see, many people fall into the trap of *splitting the difference*. Every time they counter an offer, they split the difference down the middle. I love negotiating with these people.

Instead, when you begin to negotiate price, always make smaller moves in the amount of your counteroffer.

Let's say the seller has a property on the market for $1 million. Your strike price is $965,000. You set your first offer at $910,000.

The seller says he's willing to negotiate, but you need to be more reasonable. As a show of good faith, he drops to $975,000, or $25,000 lower.

You thank the seller for negotiating, but you say that you've run the numbers and you really can't pay more than $925,000 for the property. You've just come up $15,000.

The seller comes back at $960,000 ($15,000 lower), and you counter with $935,000 ($10,000 higher).

The seller says if you can close in 60 days he will lower the price to $950,000, so he just took off another $10,000. You tell him that you can indeed close in 60 days and you'll split the difference and meet him halfway. You're at $935,000 and his last number was $950,000. Therefore the split now is at $942,500.

Let's see: You've come up from $910,000 to $942,500, or $32,500. The seller has gone down from $1 million to $942,500, or $57,500. In addition, you've gotten the deal below your strike price and both of you have given in to the other person several times.

This is not theory. It works. This one single negotiating principle can save you or make you hundreds of thousands of dollars over your lifetime with anything you negotiate in the future.

Multiple Offers

You might make three different offers simultaneously for the same property. The first could be a cash offer, the second may be a mixture of cash and terms (that is, a note to be paid later), and the third could be no cash and the seller holds a second mortgage for her equity.

The cash offer is always the lowest. Remember how you must guard your cash. Besides, if the seller gets all the goodies up front, it should be a lower offer from the standpoint of *time value of money*. You have an opportunity cost, and could have put that money to use elsewhere, making money on your money.

The second offer involves a small amount of cash at the time of closing with the rest due at a set date in the future. This is the next-highest offer.

The third offer requires none of your cash, but will be the highest number. Not only are you recognizing the seller's time value of money, but your property value should increase down the road, and you'll be in a position to share some of that wealth.

This strategy is especially useful when you buy smaller commercial properties. Be careful, though: When you buy larger commercial properties from people who've been in the game for a while, this strategy will be ineffective. Few people use it on those bigger deals.

Using the Seller's Operating Statements

This can be powerful. Let's say the seller is digging in and not budging on a price that's outside your strike price, based on the numbers you ran. Pull out the seller's own operating statements and review their contents.

Show the seller that the property wouldn't cash flow properly at the price he is asking. You explain that banks are getting stricter all the time on how much NOI you must demonstrate in relation to the debt service. This is called the *debt coverage ratio* and we discussed it earlier. It's calculated as follows:

$$\text{Debt Coverage Ratio} = \frac{\text{NOI}}{\text{Debt Service}}$$

Banks usually want to see a debt coverage ratio of 1.2 or better. This means that for every dollar of debt service you pay, you have $1.20 of net operating income.

So you say, "Mr. Seller, based on the numbers on your own operating statement, the debt coverage ratio on this deal is only 1.05. All the banks I can find will not finance the deal unless it is 1.2 or better. I figured out the price that would get us to 1.2, given the NOI of the property. That price is $X."

The seller's most common response to this statement? "Okay, if you put down more money, you'll be able to raise the ratio to where it needs to be and I don't have to come down on price."

Be prepared for that argument. Your response can then be that you are working with a group of investors, and their guidelines dictate a maximum of 20 percent down for any deal.

If all else fails, you can always look the seller straight in the eye and ask: "Mr. Seller, would *you* buy this property based on these numbers?" Then shut up.

Know When to Walk Away

We talked earlier about the *walk-away close*. That can sometimes work when you really want the deal and nothing else seems to be having an effect.

Even if you never use that close, you must be constantly prepared with a firm number in mind—*beforehand*. As you know, negotiations can get intense. If you try to do your walk-away calculation when you're emotionally charged, you will get yourself into bad deals. It's too easy to rationalize on the fly why you can offer a higher price than your strike price.

The best way to inoculate yourself from this fever is to have plenty of deals in that pipeline of yours. This is a numbers game. If you've been basing your offers on actual results and not on *pro forma* projections, then those numbers should be your solid point of reference.

You've heard of the *bigger fool theory*, in which you can always palm your deal off to someone dumber than you? Don't be the last person in that chain, who ignored the all-important strike price.

Don't Be a Weasel

I've actually heard people brag about having as many as 42 clauses in their LOIs that will allow them to get out of any deal at any time. They think they're being very clever. Everyone else just calls them *weasels*. Most companies are built on reputation. How many still-solid companies can you name that also have the reputation of being weasels?

In commercial real estate, you usually have a 30-day inspection period; occasionally it's as long as 60 days. During that period, you can leave a deal for any reason whatsoever. In that case, why should you need to add additional weasel clauses?

Purchase and Sale Agreement

After the LOI is signed by both parties, the next step is to create the *Purchase and Sale Agreement*, or *P&S*.

I have no problem having the seller draft the P&S. This saves me money, because my attorney needs only to review the draft and make any changes that he sees fit. If my attorney drafts the P&S, I'm now paying more for the entire document, but gaining no more protection.

Do not follow the advice in some investor courses, which hand you a *do-it-yourself* P&S. The theory is you only add the clauses that relate to your situation, and can now save all your money by avoiding attorney involvement.

It's the difference between my approach (saving money) and their approach (being cheap and dumb).

Every state has slightly different laws and interpretations. No single contract could ever effectively maximize your protection in every state, for every deal. Pay the bucks for an attorney who specializes in real estate investing, and let her do her job.

Hazardous Waste

In every one of your commercial contracts, you should have a hazardous waste clause. It should basically state that the seller has no knowledge of any hazardous waste on the property. This includes underground oil tanks, toxic mold, asbestos, buried asphalt shingles, and so on.

Buyers of commercial real estate are not protected by standard consumer protection laws. You must insist that the seller be clear—in writing—about what he knows or doesn't know concerning hazardous waste. Either the seller acknowledges that he knows of no hazards on the property, or you want to be informed of them prior to closing.

The lender will require that you do a *Phase One Environmental Inspection*. This covers all known forms of hazardous waste. Get a Phase

One done, even in the rare case that a bank does not require one, or you are doing a deal that doesn't involve financing. It's an insurance policy against getting stuck in a nightmare situation where you cannot resell a property.

I further discuss Phase One and Phase Two environmental inspections in the chapter on due diligence.

Overview of the Process from Here On

If you've followed my advice on attracting, analyzing, and negotiating your deal, you're likely to be in the proud position of working a live deal. We now have to turn it into a *done deal*.

We go into much detail in the coming chapters, but here's a summary of the steps coming up:

- Put down a deposit of one percent to three percent of the purchase price. Remember, you may be getting that deposit from your private lender/partners.
- Get the seller's financial due diligence package and confirm that your offer is still practical, based on all the additional information you now have. If it is not, renegotiate for a better deal. If the seller will not renegotiate, walk away.
- Start the physical due diligence and start to decide whom you will use for financing. Walk the property with your property inspector. This is the first time that you'll take money out of your pocket—money you will not get back—because you will pay for the property inspection. That's why we first do the inexpensive financial analysis, and only later do the physical analysis.
- Engage an attorney to start the title work and legal due diligence. Sign a *term sheet* with the lender with whom you will finance the deal. The lender will require a nonrefundable deposit between $7,000 and $25,000, depending on the size of the deal. This deposit pays not only for the lender's time, but also for the

appraisal, inspection, Phase One, and any other third-party reports.

- Complete all the due diligence. If it all checks out, sign off on the inspection period. Your deposit is now nonrefundable, and you may be required to put up an additional deposit.
- The lender approves the loan and sends it to the closing department at the lender's office.
- You get the funds wired, close the deal, and are now the newest member of a very exclusive community of commercial property owners!

IN THE NEXT CHAPTER

I know—you have lots of questions about whether you're getting into a truly good deal. That's completely normal, because at this stage even an experienced commercial real estate investor will be full of questions about the deal.

Fortunately, the next stage is the *due diligence period*, and it's designed to answer those questions. In the following chapter, you discover how to perform due diligence like a pro.

 AVOID A QUICK DEAL

Remember that the word *negotiation* has *ego* in it. Each participant must feel he has won a number of hard-fought concessions from his adversaries to satisfy his ego that he has done his job well.

If you are negotiating over a piece of property, go through the motions, even though you might already be satisfied with the price and terms. Because unless the other party has satisfied his ego, he is not going to make the deal, or he is going to find a reason not to close on the deal. The other party has to be convinced he is making a good deal.

From *Trump Strategies for Real Estate: Billionaire Lessons for the Small Investor* by George H. Ross, John Wiley & Sons, 2005, page 62.

6

How to Discover the Truth Behind a Deal

How to Manage the Due Diligence Process

If you're investing smart, you're investing very little time on the stream of deals that come to you when you have an effective deal-attraction machine.

Week after week, you're getting better at reviewing deals and knowing when you have a potential gem on your hands. With the letter of intent, you and the seller are taking the transaction to a serious level. You're pulling out the 80/20 rule again, but this time you'll be spending 80 percent of your time on potentially great deals.

In real estate, the 30- or 60-day period after an offer is accepted is called an *inspection period*, but the process is more commonly called *due diligence*. The term comes from Wall Street, where brokerage houses must thoroughly review a company before offering its stock to the public.

Your due diligence will be in three main phases:

1. **Financial.** Do this phase first because the other two steps require you to take money out of your pocket, and you won't be

getting it back. Besides, the numbers can quickly tell you a lot about the property.

2. **Physical.** This is where you and professional inspectors go through the property to ensure there are no major repairs or problems that you don't already know about.

3. **Legal.** Your attorneys will make sure that you receive clear title to the property and that all documents are appropriately written.

This entire process can be daunting, but I can assure you of one thing: At the end of it, you'll be either excited or relieved. You and your team may conclude that this is indeed a solid deal, and the closing will be imminent. Or you'll have realized that, based on the detailed facts about the property, you simply can't offer what the seller insists on.

Trust me: Even then it's not a total loss. You're much smarter for having gone through the process, and the next deal will go noticeably faster.

It is possible to hire companies to do the entire due diligence process for you. I suggest that you do as much as you can on your first few deals. Not only will you save money, but, more important, you'll gain

---

 AMATEUR MISTAKE: "I'LL DO IT MYSELF AND SAVE MONEY."

I don't care that you had a triple major in college of law, accounting, and construction trades. I don't care if you've done a dozen deals. If you think you can do the entire due diligence process yourself, you're crazy.

You simply can't be as good or as quick as specialists. Besides, you should seek additional pairs of experienced eyeballs to validate your impressions.

in experience and knowledge. Before you delegate, you really should know something about the task you're delegating.

Examining the Seller's Actual Numbers: The Financial Due Diligence

Your mortgage broker will be invaluable in this phase. She knows what lenders will accept and what they won't at the present moment. If she's any good, she'll also be fast. You'll know very quickly whether you still have a live one.

And it won't cost you a dime. Of course, I'm assuming you've cultivated your broker and you're not simply sending garbage over to her, expecting her to review everything the cat drags in. After you've done lots of deals and made the broker some serious money, you can think about having her review them first. For now, only run deals by your broker when you're serious about them.

This is what you will require from the seller:

- Past two years of monthly operating statements
- Year-to-date operating statement
- Rent roll for current and past two years
- Past three months of bank deposits
- Existing loan documents
- Security deposit account statement
- Utility bills
- Property tax bills
- Service contracts
- Payroll register
- Insurance policy and claim history
- Capital improvement and maintenance log
- Incomplete maintenance requests

In your purchase and sale agreement, you should require that all this information be delivered to you within 14 days from the effective date.

Insider Tip

From my experience, if the information comes in quickly, the deal usually will go smoothly. If the information comes in slowly, in little clumps, or past the 14-day deadline, you may still have a winner, but it's more likely to be a dog. It's not a reason to dump the deal yet, but a warning flag should go up in your brain.

Let's look at each of these due diligence documents:

Past Two Years of Monthly Operating Statements

These reports must show each individual month of profit-and-loss history. The months should be arranged side-by-side for a given year.

This trend report will tell you a story. If you compare the months and years, you'll undoubtedly see dips and spikes. Some of them might simply be seasonal effects. For instance, many commercial properties in a college town will reflect the ebb and flow of students and faculty during the school year.

At this point, you should simply observe and write down questions. Ideally, you'll see smooth trends in the right direction, setting aside seasonality.

Do not accept a financial statement for the past two years that is not broken down monthly. Sellers will attempt to give this to prospective buyers to hide deficiencies.

Year-to-Date Operating Statement

The past two years of operating statements will give you the most recent history of that property, but the current-year statement will tell you the present situation.

The past six months of history is the most important. This is also what the lender will focus on when deciding whether to give you the loan, how much to lend you, and at what interest rate.

This six-month period will also reveal what type of property you will be taking over. Does it have momentum, and are the numbers trending upward? That's usually the best type. Or is something happening with the property that's not allowing management to be consistent? Perhaps it's the current management itself.

Be careful of the miracle turn-around. Some properties will appear to have been going badly for the past couple of years. Then suddenly, within the past three to four months, the numbers start to look really good.

The current owner almost always will attribute it to new management. Though that may be the case, it may also be due to fluffing the numbers in preparation for a sale. For instance, there could be funny business going on with new leases that seem to be at much higher rates than usual. How could this happen?

There is a very well-known Texas retail and office developer who had a great thing going. He was so big that many other companies relied on him—an army of outside architectural, engineering, legal, and accounting firms did business with his company.

He would build a shiny new office complex and suggest that a mixture of these firms quickly sign leases at the new building. Buyers would think: "Wow—the developer was right about the prospects for that local market! It was amazing how fast that building became fully leased!"

He would then sell the property to some sucker at an extremely high price for this fully-leased building with lots of solid tenants. Three years later, that herd of tenants would all pull out and sign leases at the developer's next new property. Some scam, huh?

Be on the lookout both for problems and for situations that seem too good to be true.

Rent Roll for Current and Past Two Years

The rent roll should tell you the following for each tenant:

- Who lives in which unit
- When they moved in
- When their lease expires

- How much they pay
- Utilities charges
- Security deposit
- Amount they owe

When comparing the rent roll with the rental income line on the operating statement for any given month, the two numbers should be equal. If they are not, something is going on with the numbers.

Past Three Months of Bank Deposits

The operating statement numbers might look good, but you should verify that they are real. The past three months of bank deposits will show you what's flowing into the property account.

If they cannot show the corresponding amount of money going into the account, they probably are not collecting that money. Some sellers handle this objection by saying they are collecting cash and not putting it into the account.

Now that's kind of odd. It's possible that the seller is collecting cash, but you need to understand why. It's another red flag. If it's not a lot of money and you still want to proceed with the deal, then you want verification: Ask the seller to begin to put all future money into the account so you can verify the cash flow between now and the closing.

The deeper you look into the deal, what are you finding: more answers, or more questions? If it's the former, then things are going well. If this deal is becoming a bigger puzzle by the day, you should be worried.

Existing Loan Documents

Get a copy of all existing loan documents to see if there's any way to make this deal a little better for yourself. Perhaps the bank allows the existing loan to be assumed by a new owner. That could lower your closing costs. Again, your mortgage broker can very quickly point out any opportunities in the existing financing.

Security Deposit Account Statement

The numbers on this statement should match up with the rent roll. They better, because you will become liable for that security deposit account. When those existing tenants move out, you must give them the security deposits they put down when they became tenants.

Let's say there is not enough money in the account to cover all the security deposits. It's time to contact the seller and ask where the rest of the money is. Require that the account be completely funded prior to closing.

Utility Bills

Get copies of all utility bills for the past two years so you can match these up with the expenses on the operating statements. Some owners will say they don't have the past two years of bills. In that case, simply ask for access to go online at the utility company websites and get them, or ask for permission to talk to the utility companies. If the owner does not allow you access, something is wrong.

Property Tax Bills

Not only should you get copies of property tax bills for the past two years, but also check with the assessor's office to find out when the property will be reassessed.

Many states reassess properties at the time of closing. In most cases, property sells for a higher price than it previously sold for, so property taxes go up.

That means a dip in precious cash flow, unless you anticipated it. In fact, this one item could have a big effect on your deal.

Service Contracts

Look at all contracts with vendors who provide landscaping, parking lot maintenance, pest control, laundry facilities, elevators, pools, cable/Internet, and so on.

Also have your attorney review these contracts (in the legal phase) to know for sure which contracts are binding after the sale. You want the ability to renegotiate these contracts or cancel them after the closing.

Two contracts are almost always binding: laundry services and cable/Internet. These are typically multi-year agreements in which the seller was paid an upfront bonus for signing the deal. Such contracts are usually recorded at the registry of deeds and attached to the property.

Payroll Register

The payroll register will confirm who is getting paid what and when.

Insurance Policy and Claim History

Are there are any special stipulations in the insurance policy? Also, who is the insurer on the property? You might be able to apply to the same company and get a better rate than you would elsewhere.

Look at the claim history of the property, focusing on the number of claims and the nature of those claims. If a property has too many claims, you'll have a hard time getting insurance.

Capital Improvement and Maintenance Log

This should be an up-to-date record of all major and minor changes to the property over the past few years. If it doesn't exist, that tells you something. If it exists, but very little has been done, that also is important.

The maintenance log will indicate to you what the common problem is. Every property has one. It might be window leaks, regular cracking of the concrete, or many other issues. The log will tell you what it is, so you can anticipate this regular event both in your purchase calculations and when you take over the property.

Incomplete Maintenance Requests

This is crucial, because the number one reason your tenants will move out is if their maintenance requests are not being met.

Review the items that are still outstanding; this should provide a sense of your exposure at the time of takeover, not to mention tenant attitudes. You may find that you need to advertise heavily the message that the property is under new management and that new management cares.

If you see many requests, then make a note to yourself: If you go ahead with the deal, the first thing you must do at takeover is to have the management company visit each tenant to discuss the open items. You want the manager to be giving a specific deadline for that tenant's item to be done. Tenants are jittery enough when a property changes hands, and they're at risk of moving. This is your chance to create a *stick campaign* to keep those tenants happy and paying you monthly rent.

Tenant turnover will be your highest expense at many commercial properties, so it should be a very high priority to anticipate and solve maintenance issues.

Is Renegotiation Necessary?

You've received all the financial due diligence information. You and your mortgage broker have reviewed it. If it checks out, then it's time to take the next step.

If you've hit some surprises or discrepancies, you must now revisit your calculations. Are these new factors large enough to affect how much you can pay for the property? If so, you must go back to the seller and explain what you have found.

Some sellers will simply tell you to take it or leave it. Others will be embarrassed because their own numbers seem to contradict what you were originally told about the deal. Still other sellers had just been hoping you wouldn't figure out the right numbers, but they're willing to renegotiate, now that you know the truth.

Physical Due Diligence

You will not do much of this phase at all. You must hire a certified property inspector, who in most cases will be a civil engineer. Yes, it will cost you money, but it's well worth the price. These are professionals who know what to look for, what can be overlooked and salvaged, and what must be replaced.

Site Inspection

Do not attempt to save money by doing the site inspection yourself! It's not even a good idea with a single-family home, never mind a larger commercial property. If your deal economics cannot support the price to have professionals perform the due diligence, don't do the deal.

Physical due diligence involves the following:

- Site inspection
- Site plans and specifications
- Survey
- Tool and supply inventory
- Appraisal
- Phase I/Phase II environmental inspections
- Pest inspection
- Site inspection

This is the backbone of your physical due diligence. The purpose of the site inspection is to have your qualified engineer review all key interior and exterior components of the property to ensure they are in working order.

The inspector will check all of the structural components of the property: roof, foundation, parking lot, load-bearing walls, and so on.

Then the engineer will review the mechanical systems such as heating, air-conditioning, ventilation, electrical, and plumbing. He'll also check at least some of the interiors of units, looking for the common problems we discussed before, or anything major.

The inspection report will tell you the true physical condition of the property you are getting into. Is there a lot of deferred maintenance? Are the major mechanical systems fairly new and energy efficient, or on their last legs? How long will that roof last? Does the property comply with the Americans with Disabilities Act (ADA), and both state and local building codes? Not only will you know about any problems, but the report will also give you cost estimates of any recommended repairs.

Though I've found these estimates to be fairly accurate, engineers are not contractors. If you discover a problem that needs fixing, bring in a contractor to give you a detailed estimate.

Site Plans and Specifications

These are the documents that were used to build the property. They include building plans, floor plans, and land-use documents. You must have a copy of them for your records. If you plan any changes to the property, you will be required to produce these documents when your contractor *pulls*, or applies for, a building permit.

Survey

The survey tells you where the buildings sit on the property, where the property lines are, if the property is in a flood zone, and many other relevant details. You must have this information to determine that the property complies with various codes. You also must make sure that there are no encroachments onto the property from an adjacent landowner, and that your property does not encroach onto another site.

Get a copy of the survey from the seller, so that you and your team can be familiar with the property details. Understand, though, that your lender will require an updated survey. You may be able to save money by calling the surveyor who's listed on the blueprint and asking for an updated survey. Using the same firm can save you thousands of dollars when compared with hiring a surveyor who's unfamiliar with the property.

Tool and Supply Inventory

All tools and supplies should go with the sale. While you're on site, take an inventory of all the gear in the maintenance area, equipment in the leasing office, and any other facilities.

In fact, you would be smart to get the make, model, and serial number of each piece of substantial equipment. Sellers have been known to substitute cheap equipment and take the good stuff with them. If you make sure you know what's on the property—and someone sees you being meticulous about this—you'll have a much higher chance of seeing that equipment again when you own the property.

Appraisal

This document will largely determine the value of the property. You will not order it, because the lender will choose its own appraiser.

The appraisal must be ordered as soon as you know the property will pass your physical site inspection. It's the one item most likely to hold up your deal, because of the length of time it takes to get an appraisal done. If necessary, politely encourage your lender to get it started.

Phase I/Phase II Environmental Inspections

The lender will also order this report. As I mentioned earlier, even if you are not financing the property, you must get a Phase I done for your own peace of mind.

The Phase I report process inspects the property for all kinds of hazardous waste. It tests the water, soil, air, and materials used to construct the building. If everything looks good, the property passes. If there is a problem, then a Phase II must be done.

A Phase II is a much more in-depth report. It determines exactly the nature and magnitude of a problem, and the degree of risk involved. Plan on lenders not moving ahead until the problem is resolved.

Phase II inspections can run into tens of thousands of dollars, never mind the remediation process to fix the problem. My point is that you must always get the Phase I done on a property, so you'll never be left holding the bag on a deal that looks great when driving by, but is a toxic waste dump down below.

Pest Inspection

This is usually done with apartment buildings, and the most common pest is termites. They are in almost every state and can do major damage to a property in short order.

Tag Along for the Inspection

You should be at the property when the engineer does the inspection. This is a great time to get a good look at the major components yourself, and to ask the inspector questions about the property. The good ones will explain everything they're doing and what they find.

In an apartment complex, after the inspector examines the structural and mechanical components, he will do a survey of the units. That means doing a spot-check of perhaps 20 percent of the units, looking for substantial issues.

If the inspector finds problems, he will go into more units. If not, he will stick with the spot-check.

On the other hand, *you* must go into every unit and inspect. In part, you are looking for problems, but what you're really doing is getting a feel for the property:

- How old are the fixtures?
- What condition is the flooring in?
- Do you see mold as a result of bad ventilation?

- Are there any visible water problems near windows or on ceilings or floors?

Have a checklist with you and only mark the issues or items that must be addressed. This will save you a lot of time, compared with checking everything off, good and bad.

What If You Find a Problem?

By now you know what I'm going to say: You've completed the physical due diligence and have the inspection report, plus your own notes about the property. No property is perfect, so we're expecting some level of small problems. If that's all you are aware of, say a silent thank-you.

On the other hand, you may very well have discovered that the roof is in pretty bad shape, or that the boiler needs a $30,000 repair.

Share your findings with the seller: "Mr. Seller, you did not inform me that a problem with the boiler existed prior to my inspection. Had I known that it did, I would have reflected that in my price. My offer assumed a property in total working order. Do you feel that it would be fair to compensate me for the repairs I will have to make at closing?"

What you're asking for is a repair allowance; in other words, funds the seller gives you at the closing to cover the cost of repairs. If the seller says he won't pay a dime and will not cooperate, then you must decide just how good this deal is. You can either absorb that cost, or walk away from the deal.

Again, do not nickel-and-dime the seller about minor repairs. Reserve your negotiations for the major stuff, where you can clearly show a material difference from what you were originally told, and what you now know.

LEGAL DUE DILIGENCE

You've managed to get through the financial and physical due diligence, so there's one phase left: Now you can engage the attorney to start the legal due diligence.

Don't do this any earlier, because good attorneys are expensive. They will either ask you for a portion of their fee up front, or they may be okay with waiting to be paid at the closing. Either way, the billing meter will start to run now.

Legal due diligence involves reviewing the following:

- Title
- Building code violations
- Zoning certificates
- Insurance
- Rental ordinances
- Licenses, certificate of occupancy, and other permits
- Vendor contracts
- Estoppels
- Title inspection

Your attorney or title company will review the ownership chain of the property. That involves examining the property deed and many dusty documents in the county registrar's office. She's searching for any liens, judgments, easements, or encroachments that could affect the use and value of the property.

When a title is clouded, it means that some past owner or vendor has a dispute. These issues are not always major, but they do have to be remedied. Regardless of any assurances from the seller, never accept a property with a defective title.

Building Code Violations

Always check with the city or town for violations of building or health codes. You will be responsible for these violations as soon as you take ownership of the property.

As with everything else, sometimes these violations are major and other times they are quickly resolved. Their magnitude will determine whether you ask the seller to reimburse you in the form of a repair allowance.

Zoning Certificates

Your property must be zoned for the purpose you intend for it. Never assume that because the buildings are being used that way today, that they were approved for that use. I have the scars to prove that the past doesn't matter.

You cannot appear before a zoning board as the new owner of a property and hope to win by saying: "Well, it was a shopping center before, so I should be able to keep it going as a shopping center." All you will accomplish is to annoy these people, whose vote can either clear or kill your deal. Therefore, find out in advance what the actual zoning is.

Also see if there is multiple-use or mixed-use zoning for the property. This is always a plus: Sometimes after owning a property for a few years, the highest and best use changes to a different property type. With multiple or mixed zoning, you may not have to go before city officials and rezone.

Insurance

Get the insurance history for the property. Find out what claims have been paid or made in past years and start getting insurance rate quotes.

Sometimes it can be difficult to get commercial insurance. The first thing to try is to go to the existing insurance company. Ask what they would charge to reinsure the property under your new ownership.

Local Ordinances

Forget about common sense. You need to know exactly what ordinances your city has, relating to your property. That's another reason to hire an experienced local property management firm, which will know these rules inside-out.

Building inspectors and code enforcement officers are overworked and underpaid. That means they're on a hair trigger to become annoyed with a building owner.

Not only should you avoid annoying these people, but you should do what I suggested earlier about real estate brokers: Be easy to do business with. Treat the local officials with respect and jump to it when they give you instructions.

If you get on their good side, they can actually become sources for properties. I've done several great deals that started with a city official contacting me and wondering if I would be willing to take over a property that someone else screwed up.

On the other hand, if you get branded as a troublemaker or a smart-aleck, they can stall the process on your property and destroy your investment very quickly.

Licenses, Certificates of Occupancy, and Permits

Know which licenses, certificates, and permits you'll need by calling the local city clerk.

You'll probably need a business license, certificate of occupancy, and other miscellaneous permits to run your property. Make sure you have their expiration dates marked on your calendar! In the early days of the Internet, Microsoft almost lost one of its most important domain names because a clerk forgot to send in a renewal check for $35.

Vendor Contracts

As I mentioned before, make sure your attorney reviews all vendor contracts not only for the commitment that will apply to you as the new owner, but for any abnormal clauses. Now is the time to get explanations from the seller, and in extreme cases, to be reimbursed if the contractual obligation warrants it.

Estoppels

This is a very important item that I also referred to earlier. Retail and office tenants should fill out an estoppel letter. Your attorney will be familiar with the format. These letters are a way to audit what the seller told you. Tenants will indicate what they are paying in rent, the term of the lease, the amount of their security deposit, and which other expenses (such as utilities) they are responsible for paying.

Compare the tenants' understanding with what you were told by the seller's rent roll.

THE BIG PICTURE

As with the other due diligence phases, step back and review the results of the legal due diligence. Judge what are minor inconsistencies or findings, and what truly merits a discussion with the seller or seller's broker.

A word of caution: Your reputation is everything in this business. With each deal you do, your reputation grows—or shrinks. Do not interpret all the due diligence items here as separate opportunities to renegotiate. They're separate steps, but unless you've just uncovered a deal-breaker, you should wait until you have all the results.

You may find that the seller's records were off in her favor for most items, but that a few items are off in your favor. For instance, your engineer may report that the mechanical systems can be fixed and not replaced, thus saving you money.

Once you have all the information, you're in a position to look at your original offer and assess the big picture. With all that you now know, is that *price* still a fair deal for both parties?

Pick your battles by overlooking the small stuff and focusing only on the issues that simply cannot be ignored.

The mark of a professional is not how tough a negotiator she is; it's how good are the deals she does. The easier you are to do business with, the more *primo* deals brokers will send your way.

Once you've completed your due diligence and have looked at the big picture, notify the seller and the broker as soon as possible of your findings. Don't wait until the inspection date arrives. Your seller and broker will appreciate being notified early, and they'll remember you on that next great deal.

If you do resolve any issues, be prepared for your deposit to become nonrefundable very soon. You might even be asked to put down more nonrefundable money as you work your way to the closing.

One Very Key Step

Before you sign off on the due diligence, be sure you have a written commitment from a lending institution to finance your deal. If there are any items in the loan commitment letter that must be satisfied before the closing, now is an excellent time to make sure you'll be able to do them all.

And I do mean written commitment. I had a four-property commercial portfolio under contract in Louisiana for $12.1 million, with $130,000 down as a deposit. It was a week before the expiration of the inspection period, and the bank had not yet given me a commitment.

I kept calling my loan officer and he assured me that everything would be fine. He said the loan committee would be meeting on Thursday and that he had already received the green light from a couple of key people on the committee.

Thursday came and two of the committee members were on vacation. Now they didn't have enough members to vote, and my deal was pushed off to the following week.

I had a choice: Sign off on the due diligence and take my loan officer's word that it would be approved next week—or get an extension from the seller. I opted for the extension.

I called the seller and explained that I needed a one-week extension. He said "Hey, Dave, no problem . . . as long as you're willing put up another $65,000 hard" (that is, nonrefundable). I told him "No way." I wanted the extension, but I wasn't putting up any money hard.

He asked me to prove my confidence with the lender by putting up that nonrefundable money. I didn't trust the loan officer enough to bet $65,000 on his word. I told the seller that I wouldn't do it. The property would have to go out of contract and back on the market. When I got my loan, we could go back into contract if he wanted to.

He said "Fine," with every intention of shopping that deal, hoping for a higher price before I got my loan commitment the next week. There was nothing I could do about the situation. I had to stay protected.

One week later, the loan committee denied the loan! They said they didn't like the area in which two of the properties were located. Oh, but they might reconsider if I put more money into the down payment. I knew my strike price and cash-on-cash target. The deal would not work with more of my money, so I walked away.

I almost paid $65,000 for the lesson that you just got: Make sure you have financing lined up before you commit to moving ahead to the closing.

Getting to the Closing

You've signed off on the due diligence, and now it's a march to the closing. You must close on time or your deposit will be at the mercy of the seller. You also should close on time because that's part of your reputation. They'll know you to be a performer.

You might still be taking care of some of the loan commitment items that the lender wants done before the closing. Keep your checklist in front of you at this stage, to ensure that these items get done.

Once they're completed, the lender signs off and prepares the closing documents. You should ask to see a copy of these documents as soon as they are done. Then send them to your attorney for review. If anything is out of the ordinary, you must negotiate with the lender.

The Escrow Agent

A couple of days before the closing, the escrow agent will go into high gear.

An escrow agent is a neutral third party who facilitates the closing. This person creates the closing statements for both the buyer and seller. She also handles the earnest money deposit, loan documents, and closing fees that are associated with the title transfer.

The escrow agent will obtain title insurance, pay off any outstanding liens, cut checks to any other parties, and record the property deed after the closing.

Should You Get Title Insurance?

Title insurance protects you against any defect in the title that might be pointed out during your ownership of the property. You might be thinking: "Hey, I just paid the attorney to check the title and he told me it was clear."

What if the attorney missed something? What if someone puts in a claim at a later date for a matter that the attorney could not have seen at the time?

Some years ago I negotiated a nice deal and was moving ahead to the closing. I had done the due diligence, my checklist was empty, the loan commitment was in place, and the title came back clean.

I was two days away from the closing when I got a call from the local police department, asking if I was about to purchase the property in question.

I said "Yes." The detective asked me for the seller's name and I gave it to him. He then informed me that this person did not own the property, and that the actual owner lived in Florida and knew nothing about the sale!

The police had discovered that my seller had falsified a deed and recorded it at the registry of deeds, transferring the property into his name.

When my attorney did the title search, the transfer looked clean. In fact the attorney certified that the title was clean!

Another lesson for you: Attorney certifications are not the same as title insurance. You might get a heart-felt apology from the attorney, but the only way you'll get your money back is if you first obtain title insurance.

Setting Up the Closing

When is the best time to close on your property? There are two schools of thought: Some investors like to close late in the month so they have less pre-paid interest to deal with.

I like to close at the beginning of the month. The seller is responsible for giving you all of the rent owed for the remainder of that almost-full month. If you close on the third of the month, the seller will owe you 27 days of rent from each tenant, whether he's collected it or not.

This money can come in handy if you are tight on funds going into the closing. The drawback is that you'll have more prepaid interest to pay on your loan. In my experience, the amount of rent is much higher than the amount of prepaid interest. Close early when you have the choice.

One extra benefit with commercial properties is that you don't need to go the city in which the property is located in order to close the deal. The escrow agent will send you a copy of the buyer's closing statement for your review. If you're okay with it, you sign and return it. If not, you make the necessary changes.

Be sure you read this document closely and focus on the prorations. Those are items such as taxes that must be paid by the seller up to a certain date, at which point you take them over. The same is true with rental income, as I mentioned before. Quite often there will be a mistake in the proration section. What a surprise: The mistake is almost never in your favor. If you do not detect the mistake, you eat it.

The escrow agent will also send you a copy of the closing documents. Immediately send these to your attorney for review. Now is the time to find and fix any discrepancies. Once the attorney gives the okay, you sign all the documents in front of a notary public and send them to the escrow agent. You can find notaries in the phone book, and at many insurance companies, mortgage broker offices, and banks.

While you're pushing all this paper, the seller is doing the same. All parties usually sign and send the documents back to the escrow agent by overnight delivery. Just make sure your packet goes by some method you can track, and that will include delivery confirmation.

On the scheduled day for the closing, your only official duty is to wire the funds to the escrow account. Once received, as long as no last-minute surprises develop, the escrow agent transfers the deed to you and you're the proud owner of that property.

What Should Be in Place on Closing Day

Though you've been intensely focused on getting the closing to occur, you should have already been planning for the future. On the day you take over the property, hit the ground running.

The most important thing to have done already is decide which company will manage your property. You might hire the existing company if you were impressed during the due diligence phase. On the other hand, the present management might be the first item you will replace.

Whatever you do, be sure to interview three candidates for the job and select the most qualified. Do not select based solely on price. Also do not try to talk these companies way down on price. The management company is the key player on your team. By being too cheap up front, you are only weakening their service, and you will pay dearly in lost cash flow.

You already should have received your professionally made signs, banners, and other marketing materials for the property.

Because you were monitoring all key equipment at the property, you already know if the leasing office and other facilities are fully equipped. If not, you've bought what you need, like computers, fax machines, and copiers.

You must change into the name of the new ownership entity all utilities: electric, gas, water, sewer, trash, phone, and cable.

You already have set up key accounts with either existing or new vendors for building supplies, janitorial, landscape, parking lot maintenance, alarm service, and so on. Of course your management company may be way ahead of you on this, but just make sure it got done. You're the manager of the management company.

You should have created your own budget for running the property. Your marketing plan will detail the steps to take in order to fill any vacant units, keep the desirable tenants, and eventually replace the others. You'll know the type and frequency of reports to expect from your management company

Get an up-to-date list of employees, including their salaries and responsibilities. Have a new, local bank account already set up for the property operating account, which will be used to pay vendors and other regular expenses.

On the day of takeover, you should also be working with your management company to have:

- Current rent schedule
- Security deposit report
- Pre-paid item report
- Confirmation of rent delinquencies
- Copies of any pending litigation

Discuss any changes in staff hours, and make sure the rent roll and budget are already input into the reporting system.

Make sure the manager contacts all tenants, delivering take-over letters so that they know the building has been sold, and to whom they should make out future lease checks.

Change the office locks and make sure the answering machine offers a brand-new message.

If you ensure that all this happens, you'll be running this new investment like a real pro.

In the Next Chapter

By this point in the book, I want you to have a pretty clear picture of the entire process, beginning from where you are right now, all the way to owning a commercial property.

You and I both know that I've only summarized the process, though. There are lots of details that must be attended to, and a few minefields to navigate.

In the next chapter, I discuss risk. We step back from the nitty-gritty of closing details, and again look at the big picture. I explain the variety of acceptable risks that come with being in the real estate business, and what additional risks you can avoid entirely.

7

TAKE ONLY
INTELLIGENT RISKS

I won't insult your intelligence by saying: "Real estate investing involves risk." You know that, having read this far.

I won't even say, "The goal is to take as little risk as possible." That's also too simplistic, because it turns risk into the objective when you and I both know we're in real estate with the objective of making money.

Instead, our goal should be to eliminate all unnecessary risk, and understand the risk we do take on. That's what I mean by "Take only intelligent risks."

I see it happen all the time to certain investors who are long on enthusiasm and very short on preparation. First they get all excited about investing. Then they dive in and flail around for a while. A few get lucky and their first deal actually works out okay. However, most of these investors get out of real estate as fast as they got in. For decades to come, they'll then proclaim to anyone who will listen that "I tried real estate investing and it doesn't work."

It doesn't have to be that way. In this chapter I show you how to avoid many of the career-ending mistakes investors make. That's the part about eliminating all unnecessary risk. I'll also explain what can go wrong and why. That way, you'll be moving ahead with the confidence of knowing what to expect.

CRUCIAL ELEMENTS OF YOUR SUCCESS

Whatever you do, don't get caught in the *chicken-and-egg* quandary of "I can't get good at real estate investing unless I do deals, but how can I hope to do a decent deal until I'm somewhat good at this whole business?"

I have great news. You get good by doing three things:

1. Look at lots of deals.
2. Realize that your early negotiations with sellers are not binding.

Taking the first two steps will then allow you to:

3. Make offers regularly.

Let's now look at each of these elements.

LOOK AT LOTS OF DEALS

When you begin to analyze deals, your goal should not be to get a deal done as soon as possible, strange as that advice may seem. I figure that you want to be in this business for the long term, so my most important early objective is to get you the strongest, most stable foundation for investing.

You do that by analyzing as many deals as you possibly can. The old advice works great here: *Practice makes perfect.* It's only through seeing deal after deal that you get a feel for how the numbers work.

At first, everything's new to you. But the more deals you see, the faster you're moving up the learning curve. Soon you will begin to see things:

- Wow, I've never seen a deal with expenses this high.
- I've looked at eight deals in that part of town and this is the first one that has a cash-on-cash return over 10 percent.

- I'm beginning to see that retail space in strip malls these days is running in this range . . . why does this deal have such low rates?

What you're doing is observing, comparing, and above all, asking questions.

The wonderful thing about this process is that it can happen as quickly as you want it to. If your marketing machine is well-built and humming, you'll be seeing deal after deal.

In fact, you can go to www.loopnet.com and begin to see deals five minutes from now. It's true that most of them will not be what you're after. That's okay, because you're just getting comfortable at this stage. Sailors get their *sea legs*, and you're getting your *deal legs*.

As I mention in an earlier chapter, begin to build relationships with brokers just as soon as you can. When doing so, understand that initially you will be tested. The broker will send you a few deals to see if you will take the bait. These are usually deals the broker hasn't been able to sell to anyone else. He's not only sizing up your knowledge, but, who knows—you just might take the deal off his hands.

Even the *dog deals* can be helpful to you. You'll be able to analyze that many more deals, and you will have an opportunity to build rapport with the broker. To make that happen, it's crucial that you handle the dog deals properly. Here are your options:

Option 1: Silence. You simply don't say anything. This is unprofessional. You must thank the broker for sending you anything, and use that opening as a chance to explain what you're looking for.

Option 2: Call the broker and say: "Mr. Broker, why did you send me that piece of junk? You know as well as I do that those numbers just don't work. I'm not stupid, you know." This is an excellent way to never hear from the broker again.

Option 3: Call the broker and say: "Mr. Broker, thank you for sending me that deal. Unfortunately, those numbers do not fit my criteria for buying. For a deal to work for me, I need a minimum cash-on-cash return of 10 percent. What do you have in your pipeline that might fit my criteria?"

You've just thanked the broker for sending you a deal, even if it's no good. That's showing professional courtesy, and it will set you apart from most of the people on his list. What you've also done is to start training the broker on the type of deals you're looking for.

You're now above all the amateurs who call the broker on a regular basis and say "Hey, you got any good deals for me?" When you follow my approach to brokers, you'll begin to see better and better deals.

At First, It's Just a Date

If you take the attitude when dating that each time is an important commitment, you're most likely going to die single. Instead, on early dates you are simply getting to know each other better.

Let's say you look at a deal and decide that it has some merit. You get to know each other by making an offer, in the form of your letter of intent (LOI). You're simply asking for a date, with no commitments. That leads us into the third and final step in getting good at real estate investing:

Make Offers Regularly

You should actively strive to put in as many LOIs as you can. It's crucial that you get the feel of going through the process. When you talk with the broker or seller about a deal, you get to experience the start of the negotiation process.

I want to be crystal clear: Even when the numbers are not close, you should still create an LOI and submit it! You won't be doing this during your entire career, but you should focus on it at first. Remember, you're getting your deal legs.

Don't simply write up any deal. Do first try to analyze the numbers and rate the potential of the opportunity. My point is to make sure you don't let lack of quality prevent you from making regular offers.

So write up your LOI. Then do not just fax it over blindly to the broker or seller. Instead, call the seller and say:

> Mr. Seller, I'm about to fax you over an LOI for your Main Street property. I want you to know that I've analyzed the numbers and my offer will come in much lower than the asking price. As a matter of fact, based on the numbers that I was given and my need to have a 10 percent cash-on-cash return going into the deal, my offer will be X dollars. I know it is much lower than the asking price—should I fax over the offer?

The other party will start asking you questions. This will give you the experience of answering questions about the deals you're making offers on. The more you do this, the more confidence and momentum you'll create for yourself, and the more relationships you will be developing.

From time to time, the answer will be "Yes, fax it over." Great! Now you'll be negotiating with absolutely no risk on your part. Will you be asked questions you can't answer? Yes. So what? Anyone in this business has been in that position, so it's not a big deal.

You'll also have a great experience from time to time, when one of these low-ball offers is accepted!

HOW TO RECOGNIZE A BAD DEAL EARLY IN THE PROCESS

Now that you are on a quick learning curve, analyzing deals and making offers, it's important to manage your time properly. After all, my system is all about getting into real estate while you still have a day job. If it works in that situation, imagine how well it will work when you are your own boss someday!

When you're making offers and analyzing counter-offers, the sooner you can recognize a problem and estimate its size, the more efficient you will become. You'll spend less time on the low-payoff deals and gravitate toward the ones with serious potential.

Let's talk about the main reasons for deals to fall apart:

Bad Numbers

I know that I just finished telling you to make offers and not sweat the fact that some of those deals are crummy. That is so you get out there and acquire your *deal legs*.

Now I'm going to tell you something that appears to contradict what I just said: Dump the deals when the numbers don't work.

Here's the trick: Be sure you're out there making offers and not dumping them too soon. But when you realize that a seller will not come down on price, or will not give you great financing to counteract the high price, it's time to pass on that deal.

Remember to make a courtesy call to the seller or broker and explain your reasoning.

No Numbers

As you know from an earlier chapter, when you ask for *numbers*, you mean something specific. You want actual numbers from the past two years, plus year-to-date profit-and-loss statements. What if the seller says "I don't have those"?

Believe it or not, you will hear that occasionally. At times I've been told that the seller simply doesn't keep such records, which might be true in some cases. I've known sellers to say they just hired a new management company and the old company took all the records. That may be an excuse or it may be true.

I've never been able to put a deal together unless the seller could give me accurate statements.

Pro Forma Numbers

As you know, these numbers are merely projections and wishful thinking about what the property might do in the future. If all you receive is pro forma numbers, this is a big red flag.

The owner is saying, in effect, "I didn't run my business efficiently. If I had, I would be able to show you actual numbers this good. But don't let that stop you from paying me as if I had performed this well!"

How crazy is that? Yet you will hear this argument from seller after seller.

Pro forma numbers are fine; just don't base your price on them. If you go for bank financing, the lender will not finance you based on those made-up numbers.

Want a blazing red flag? When the seller will not give you actual numbers until you put in an offer based only on the pro forma numbers. Perhaps he thinks you'll fall for that swindle, but I know you won't.

Bad Property

The numbers may actually look good, but they also may be hiding a real headache of a property.

Perhaps the numbers are great for a good reason: The property may have a large amount of deferred maintenance. If all the mechanical and other systems are old, it may be prohibitively expensive to maintain it.

Such properties can work, but I recommend that you stay away from them until you've done many deals. At that point, you will have the experience and resources to take on a really big challenge, for a correspondingly big reward.

Wrong Area

There's an old-but-good principle in real estate: Your house should be the worst one in the neighborhood. If it's the best one, then the neighborhood will drag down the value of your house. You want those neighbors bringing up your value instead.

The same is true with commercial property. Are you considering a strip mall that has mid-level stores while the property down the street just rented to a dollar store and a teenage game arcade? This neighborhood is changing in the wrong way.

Pretty soon, your target property will lose its higher-end tenants. Then the only tenants you'll be able to rent to will be lower-end ones for lower rents. Lower rents very quickly decrease the value of your property.

All properties are classified from *A* to *D*, and so are all areas. Avoid doing business in the *D* areas. They can be highly profitable, but are even more highly management-intensive. That's another game you can play in a few years.

You're much better off avoiding all the headaches by investing in a *C* property. This property will not be pretty, but will contain tenants who provide steady income.

Properties That Have Been on the Market for a Long Time

The real estate market is just too active to let gems lie around for long. If a property's been on the market for a long time, your antenna should be active, scanning for something wrong with it.

Remember the gauntlet of buyers that a broker will contact to sell a property: First she will call her private list of best buyers; then the rest of her list will hear about it; and last of all, her office colleagues—and their own lists—will have an opportunity to buy it.

If the property still doesn't move, it will be advertised on the Internet and in the newspaper classified section.

After all these eyes review a property, the chances are very low that it's a great deal. I have found excellent properties that have been picked-over by countless earlier investors, but it's rare.

Do Not Fall into This Trap

I just finished saying that the chances are low—but not zero—of finding a good deal that's been on the market for a long time. However, do not use *low chances* as a reason for inaction!

Some people are so fearful of actually doing a deal that they talk themselves out of good ones. They look for reasons not to proceed, so they won't have to face their fears.

I went through that phase. When I started investing, it took me a few months to piece together the knowledge I needed to do that first deal. The learning process was nice, comfortable, and nonthreatening. As soon as I had that knowledge, fear began to take over. I was afraid to do my first deal. It was mostly fear of the unknown, coupled with an overactive imagination.

As I analyzed deals, I found myself looking for reasons why a deal wasn't a deal. You know what? I could *always* find a reason . . . or two or five.

For nine long, unprofitable months I allowed myself to do this. I then found a property whose numbers really worked. In my fear paralysis, I just couldn't bring myself to put in an offer. I did what's called *bird-dogging*: I gave that lead to another investor for a small fee. At least I had taken some action and made some money, I told myself. The truth was that I had simply avoided doing the deal.

That investor was so busy doing other deals that he let his offer expire. I bird-dogged the same deal to someone else, but he was too busy. So was the third investor.

I knew this property was a deal. With no other excuses handy, I swallowed hard and bought my first deal.

I'm here to tell you that just one little deal makes all the difference! I realized that the oceans did not rise up to swallow me, and I still had a pulse . . . and a deal.

Well then! Only three months later I had three more properties. After six months I had done nine deals. Within one year of confronting my fears I had eleven deals under my belt. There is nothing better than taking action and getting over the hurdle of doing that first deal.

If you catch yourself looking for reasons not to do deals, get yourself an experienced partner to assist you with your first one. That will give you the confidence to spread your wings and start doing your own.

Amateur Mistake: "I gotta do this deal!"

This syndrome happens for a variety of reasons, all of them bad: You might still be waiting to do your first deal, and fear has been replaced by desperation.

Or it could be that you've already invested in a few properties, but this one looks like a trophy to you. Maybe a rival investor is bidding on it, or perhaps it's a well-known property in your town and you fantasize about strolling into a meeting and announcing that you own it.

When you feel as though you absolutely must do a deal, step back and get an objective opinion. Otherwise, here's what the *slippery slope* looks like:

You get the numbers from the seller. Yes, they're pro forma numbers, but wow do they look good! According to the seller, there's a *big* payday at the end of this deal for you, and you start to taste it.

The seller asks you simply to put in an offer pending the compilation of the actual numbers. "Once we agree on a price, I'll be more than happy to release all the numbers to you," he says.

You come to terms, and you're pumped—the seller agreed to take 10 percent less than the asking price!

When you get the actual numbers, you're not so pumped. There are potential problems. The income is up and down like a seesaw, and the pro forma numbers are based on the best months. He very confidently assures you that with good management, the property can easily perform at that level consistently.

You notice that expenses are much higher than reported. The seller has a ready explanation: He is paying for all of the utilities, but you can submeter the property and have tenants pay for utilities going forward. That will give you a windfall of cash, he explains.

You're hungry for a deal, what he's telling you sounds good, and he seems like a real honest guy.

Even your management company agrees that it can keep the property performing at the level that the seller had in his best months (they will tell you this to impress you). They also agree that it's possible to submeter the utilities and collect more from tenants.

(*Continued*)

AMATEUR MISTAKE (*CONTINUED*)

You do the deal.

Right off the bat, your management company is not able to hit that best-month level of income. They do come close at times, but they miss on other months, and the shortfalls happen more frequently.

When you prepare to submeter the property, you realize that you can't require the tenants to pay utilities until their leases expire. This results in another income gap.

When you finally start to raise the rents, you notice something: Some tenants decide to move out instead of paying the higher utility bills. You come to learn that your main competition pays the utilities, and their properties are younger.

You're now not only losing tenants, but new ones are not attracted to your property, which has that competitive disadvantage. Your cash flow drops because you have lower occupancy. Your property value goes down with it.

One day the floodgates in your mind open and you wonder why you ever decided to invest in commercial property in the first place. You wonder if that accounting job is still open down at the plant.

It could all have been avoided. A deal must work based on actual numbers . . . period. As soon as you find yourself rationalizing how you can "make this deal work," you need to dump it and move on to the next one. The only thing that you *"gotta"* make is rational buying decisions to increase your wealth.

KNOW WHERE YOU ARE IN THE REAL ESTATE CYCLE

You must always know this when buying a property. Remember, you're not just buying into a property, but also into a market.

How is the local market doing?

Are new jobs coming in, and are even more projected to come in?

How is the supply?

How many permits were pulled in the past couple of years for the same type of property you are buying?

How many of those properties are being built near your property? If the number is higher than average, you now have another question to answer: Is the market becoming oversupplied, or is it growing so fast that the absorption far exceeds supply?

Is there any vacant land near your property that could be built on?

Have there been any recent announcements that jobs were leaving the area?

What have rents been doing for the past couple of years? Have they been stagnant or rising, or are they just starting to rise after years of weakness?

These are all important questions to ask about a market before you enter it. The answers will determine your exit strategy and your buying parameters.

If you've been in a market that's had a long *run-up*, or increase, you know that it will soon be oversupplied. In that case, your exit strategy should be to hold nothing in this market. Instead, you should buy the property and quickly sell to another buyer so that you get into a cash position. Cash will be king in the coming down-market in that area.

What if you have a *killer deal*, and you hate the thought of just flipping it? Consider flipping it and when the market rolls over, pick up the same killer deal for less, six to eight months later.

If you do buy that deal at the peak of the market, get ready for it to look not so killer for a while. You're going to have to hold it while the market declines and eventually rebounds. It's generally not a good idea to do this, because your money will be tied up for a long time. During that period you will have missed the opportunity to make faster, more profitable plays elsewhere.

Don't Let Yourself Be the Cause of Failure

This usually happens in one of three ways:

1. Not taking action
2. Being cheap
3. Doing marginal deals

Not Taking Action

It's easy to see something that's not right with your deal and ignore it. Perhaps you want to wait a while and see if the problem corrects itself, or maybe you're just being lazy. Either way, problems generally tend to get worse.

The other form of nonaction that can cause failure is to overanalyze a deal. Yes, you're *taking action* of sorts by crunching the numbers over and over. The problem is, I define action as *making offers*. As we discussed earlier, you must guard against never getting around to making those offers.

Being Cheap

Some people try to save money on the property inspection by doing it themselves. That's plain crazy. No matter how well you've been able to insulate yourself and really focus on the numbers, down deep you're much more emotionally tied to the deal than an inspector is.

Besides, you're not qualified! I'm a licensed general contractor with many hundreds of projects under my belt, and *I am not qualified*, okay? So what does that make you?

Get a local professional with years of experience. That person knows the local and state laws, the neighborhood, and quite possibly even your target property. Just one sentence from this person can save you tens of thousands of dollars in trouble down the road.

Don't try to save money on attorneys, either, by hiring a relative, friend, or a general-practice attorney. Commercial real estate attorneys *are* expensive. It's a cheap form of insurance, though, to keep you out of bad deals and protect you in the deals you do invest in. If it makes you feel any better while you write out those checks, remember two things: You should only get into deals that are good enough to support the additional costs of attorneys and other team members. Also, your attorney can become a great source of future deals, thus earning you much more than the fees cost you.

Another great way to get yourself into trouble is by being cheap with your property. When repairs arise, *do them*. When tenants have maintenance problems, mandate that your property manager jump on the matter.

The number-one reason for tenants to leave your building is a lack of response to maintenance problems. They won't be leaving because of the rent.

I'm not only advocating that you react quickly, but recommending that you become proactive. Have a program to identify deferred maintenance on your property regularly. When you continuously correct wear and tear, your property will always look good and your tenants will notice the care that you demonstrate, in comparison with your cheapskate competition.

Once your retail or office tenants start getting remarks about the property from outside sources, you're in trouble. Now you've affected the image of other businesses as well, and you will pay dearly for that. Not only will the tenants move out as soon as is practical, but leasing the space will become much harder.

Then the downward spiral picks up speed. You hold on for a couple of months without anyone filling that vacant space, and then you lower the lease rate. You're also deferring more maintenance because cash flow has dried up. You eventually get a tenant who is willing to pay the lower rate, but it's not a tenant that adds to the image of your property. That drives out more tenants, and so on.

You try to bail out by selling, and are shocked to discover that the value of your property has dropped so far that it has *fallen out of bed*, as they say on Wall Street. The cure for this slippery slope? Keep that property well-maintained at all costs.

Doing Marginal Deals

There's nothing exactly wrong with a marginal deal. You might be working off actual numbers, with a property that's well maintained in an acceptable area. The only problem is that it's a *squeaker* of a deal.

Marginal deals have numbers below ten percent cash-on-cash return. I know I've mentioned this target number before. Some investors will think I'm crazy to expect to get a ten-percent minimum cash-on-cash return to get into a deal. Some realtors and owners may even tell you that it is impossible to get such a return in their area.

Let them talk, but don't listen to them. These people are speculators. I have nothing against speculators, but I don't believe in doing business that way. Maybe I'm *old school*, because I believe that Cash Flow Is King.

Speculators can and do make huge chunks of money, as do we more conservative investors. The difference is that speculators bet on appreciation. They are willing to live with very little cash flow. In fact, they'll sometimes buy a property with negative cash flow with the hope of that *big payday* down the road.

Speculating is similar to investing on the basis of pro forma numbers: If the market takes a sudden shift from that hoped-for trend, the speculator now must hold the property for an extended period.

Contrast that strategy with investing for cash flow. If the market suddenly shifts on me, I simply have less cash flow. I like that better.

Little or No Traffic

Traffic is known as a *leading indicator*. In other words, when traffic is strong, it results in other things being strong, such as sales. The reverse is also true.

Be wary of properties that are hard for customers to get to, or that do not have enough traffic to support them. As I mentioned earlier, traffic can vary significantly from one side of the street to the other, or one block to the next.

Some commercial investors make a point of noticing where the *big boys* like McDonald's® and Starbucks® locate their stores. It's called the *follow-that-cab approach*, and it can work very well. These companies have site selection down to a science, and you may be able to benefit from that. At the very least, try to notice everything you can about where they locate their properties. Nothing is accidental with them.

When Good Debt Turns into Bad

Turn on your TV late at night and you'll hear another *no-money-down* pitch for real estate investing. I've already explained that although most of these deals are not good, it is possible to invest in good properties with *no money of your own down*. In other words, they are regular deals that require down payments, but you get a lender to put up the down payment.

I discuss financing in more depth in the next chapter, but I want to make a point about risk here: Just because you *can* arrange lots of debt on a deal does not mean that you necessarily *should*.

Debt has a way of eating up cash flow, and the danger arises when your deal is thin on cash flow to begin with. When those funds must go to debt service, you're taking a big risk.

Think of cash flow after debt service as your safety net. That's the amount of excess dollars that ideally go into your pocket, but could be used for the property. For instance, if the property needs additional repairs or occupancy temporarily dips, having that cash flow is a great way to smooth out the ups and downs.

When you have a deal that works on paper with lots of debt and very little cash flow, it starts to look a lot like the pro forma deals I mentioned earlier. You had better be exactly right in your projections, or bad things will quickly begin to happen to your investment.

Remember the *debt coverage ratio*:

$$\text{Debt Coverage Ratio} = \frac{\text{Net Operating Income}}{\text{Debt Service}}$$

Regardless of the amount of debt you can arrange, shoot to have a debt coverage ratio of 1.25 or higher. That will ensure that you have adequate cash flow to cover your operating expenses and debt service.

When banks finance you, they will require that your debt coverage ratio be 1.20 or better in good times, and around 1.25 in lean times. It's also a good rule of thumb for you to use, even if you're not financing through banks.

Don't Persuade Yourself into Failure

I already talked about the dire consequences of ignoring deferred maintenance. Here are three other situations that you absolutely must stay on top of:

1. Collections
2. Occupancy
3. Attitude

Collections

It's realistic to expect your management company to have a few outstanding rents in the first part of the month. However, they should be *zeroing out* by the end of the month. In other words, they should have collected all rents by then.

I'm not suggesting that tenants be told they have until the end of the month. Instead, I'm referring to your internal reporting standard. If you're not at 100 percent, you must be on top of the situation. It's your job to manage the manager.

Even with the goal of 100 percent collections by the end of the month, it's common to have up to three percent in delinquent rents. Just make sure the manager is actively pursuing these tenants. Rents that go uncollected for more than thirty days are likely to go uncollected permanently.

Occupancy

The first job of your management company is to fill up the property. The second job is to collect rents, and the third job is to keep that property full. Your biggest expense will be tenant turnover.

Occupancy should at least equal the average current occupancy for properties of your type in your market. If it's lower, the management company is not doing a good job. If it's higher, then you picked a good company.

When the first of the month comes and you don't have a tenant filling a unit, that income is lost forever. To avoid this bleak situation, you must have a strong tenant retention program.

The first element of that program is to ensure maintenance is quickly taken care of. Insist that the manager call the tenant and acknowledge the request. Then, the service standard should be to fix the problem within 24 hours, and preferably the same day. If it's an emergency, then of course you need immediate response.

After the maintenance is complete, tenants should get another call to ask if they are satisfied with the work. If they are not, the work must be quickly attended to. If they are, then you've just turned a maintenance request into a positive impression of your property.

I want to stress again that it's not enough to be a quick reactor to tenant issues. You should insist that your manager be proactive. They should be continually watching for issues and fixing them whether tenants complain or not. Now you're *really* earning goodwill.

Attitude

This item will directly affect your profit-and-loss statement. As corny as it may sound, everyone on your team must have a *can-do* attitude. It must be on display when leasing the property, dealing with tenants, and interacting with contractors.

I was in the midst of a large repositioning project a while back. The first management company was highly skilled. Unfortunately, the skill was related to hiding its inefficiency. By the time I discovered this, the company had cost me a lot of time and money.

Needless to say, I hired another firm. After a couple of months, I made a visit to the site, in part to talk with the manager. I was not happy with the occupancy rate or the way that the company was accounting for costs. I met with the manager and the lead maintenance person to go over goals for the next 30 to 90 days. As I set one goal, I saw the manager look at the maintenance man and roll her eyes.

I knew right then that my property would be in trouble if she remained as manager. I voiced my concern to the management company. To make a long story short, she soon *decided to pursue other opportunities*, as they say. Soon my property was thriving.

An executive at Nordstrom—the store that's famous for its great customer service—was once asked how it managed to train such excellent people. He replied that it had long ago given up focusing mainly on training, and instead focused on finding people whose attitude was already great. Yes, Nordstrom also provided training , but it had no illusions about training being able to turn a poor attitude into a good one.

BE THE *RIGHT* KIND OF CONTROL FREAK

The wrong kind is the *do-it-yourselfer*. This person may be too cheap to hire good talent or may think he can do a better job than anyone else. Whatever the reason, it's a prescription for mediocrity and burnout.

You must let go, and you must do so sooner than you think is appropriate. Even when you have very little money, you should be looking for ways to delegate easy tasks to family members, or to low-cost helpers from the local elderly center.

As I mentioned earlier, you must only be doing deals that can support the involvement of professional specialists such as mortgage brokers and property managers.

In a later chapter, I discuss the kind of team you must create. What I want to stress here is that your goal should not be to do the work yourself, but instead to control the specialists who do the work for you.

It's lucky for you that an excellent way to invest is also an excellent way to learn the art of delegation: Buy a property that's a couple of hundred miles away in an emerging market—much too far away for you to be dropping by frequently. You'll then have to discover how to manage a good management company.

Once you get the hang of it, you'll never go back! You'll be set free from your local market, and will be able to invest wherever the best opportunities are.

Back to your management company: You must channel your hands-on attitude toward the thorough review of certain key pieces of information that you should get every week. Here's what your *Monday Morning Report* should tell you:

- Current occupancy
- The past week's occupancy
- Projected 30-day occupancy
- Projected 60-day occupancy
- Number of move-ins projected
- Number of make-readies completed in the past week
- Number of make-readies projected for this week
- Number of work orders requested
- Number of work orders completed
- Number of potential tenants who inquired about leasing
- Number of new applicants
- Number of new leases
- Amount collected for the month
- Amount delinquent for the month

This report gives you a snapshot of where the property is right now, and where it's likely to be 30 to 60 days from now.

Because you are looking ahead a couple of months, but doing so every week, you should catch issues quickly and have time to remedy them.

Another point about management companies: Make sure that your management contract can be terminated with no longer than 60 days' notice. Do not sign yearly contracts, or your leverage over a bad management company will diminish.

THREE TYPES OF RISK

In any real estate transaction, there will be different amounts of three types of risk.

Business Risk

This stems from making poor business decisions. They could be your judgments, for example, when you hire the wrong management company and your income suffers because of it.

Your management company, in turn, may be making bad judgments in the form of ineffective tenant screening and inconsistent rent collection practices.

In either case, it's important to recognize these errors early on and fix them quickly.

Financial Risk

This relates to the borrowed funds used to purchase the property.

We already discussed the risk of over-leveraging your property. It's important to consider the amortization of the debt, too—in other words, how the debt will be paid off.

Most commercial loans feature a balloon payment. For example, you may arrange for a loan that has payments calculated as if it will stretch over 25 years. That would be 25-year amortization. However, the loan would include a balloon payment somewhere between five to ten years from inception. Let's say it's seven years: In that case, the first seven years of the loan would have relatively low payments, as if it were to take 25 years to pay off. Then, in year seven, all remaining principal will come due.

This form of financing results in more manageable payments during those seven years. The risk is that, at the end of the balloon period, you do not have the money to pay off the note. There are many reasons why you may not have the full amount: For example, the value of the property may actually decline rather than increase in seven years' time.

You may even owe more on the property than it's now worth. If this is the case, you will have to sell the property and come to the closing with additional money out of your own pocket. Not good.

If property values have not tanked, you do not necessarily have to sell the property at the end of seven years. It's common to refinance the loan, paying off the original debt and putting in place perhaps another balloon mortgage.

Insurable Risk

You can insure your property against a whole family of risks, including flood, fire, and storms. Insurance policies also include manmade situations, such as being sued by tenants or employees for accidents that they claim occurred on your property.

This is a *cleaner* type of risk, because you can simply buy the insurance to protect yourself. Insurance companies will base the cost of that coverage on the statistical probability of your claiming a loss, based on large amounts of historical data.

DIVERSIFICATION

Fortunately, you have several tools at your disposal to minimize these three forms of risk. The primary tool is diversification.

It's been said that the worst number in business is the number *one*. If you have only one supplier and that company implodes, you're in trouble. If you have only one product, or only one property, then you are pinning too much on that one source of your livelihood.

In real estate, it's prudent to diversify by property type and location. When the economy is soft and retail is suffering, it's often the very time when multi-family properties take off. After all, job losses often result in foreclosures, and apartments become a fall-back choice for housing.

Similarly, when one part of the country loses manufacturing jobs to overseas factories, another part of the country is booming with oil industry jobs.

Market research also reduces your risk. The more knowledgeable you are about the region, city, and property, the fewer surprises you'll have. That comes back to the quality of your network of relationships.

In the Next Chapter

If you are not scared off by all my descriptions of mistakes and risks, then you really are different from the amateurs who prefer their truth to be sugar-coated.

You deserve a change of pace, in the form of good news: A vast mechanism exists for financing your deals, and banks are only one small part of it. Turn to the next chapter and discover how your investing life can be made easier through the prudent application of other people's money.

8

USE A MONEY
MULTIPLIER

 AMATEUR MISTAKE: "THE BEST DEALS ARE
THE NO-MONEY-DOWN ONES."

I remember getting a call from a very excited student one afternoon. "Dave, did you get a chance to look at that great office building deal I sent you?"

"Yes, Paul, I did. It doesn't cash flow."

"I know, Dave, but I can get in with no money down!"

"Great. Then you'll have the pleasure of paying out of your own pocket every month to keep this deal afloat."

Getting into a deal with the main feature of *no money down* is similar to buying a car based on the amount of the rebate you'll receive on day one. At best, these elements are a superficial measure of quality. At worst, the feature is masking deeper problems with the deal.

In case you jumped ahead to this chapter, I'll repeat a key point: The best commercial deals almost always require that a substantial down payment be made. Fortunately, the payment doesn't have to come from your own pocket.

That's where your relationships again come into play; this time with *money partners*. Your lender will lend whatever its guidelines allow, and your money partners can put up most or all of the rest. We discuss this more later in the chapter.

(Continued)

AMATEUR MISTAKE (CONTINUED)

ANOTHER AMATEUR MISTAKE: "DEBT IS BAD; I ONLY BUY WHEN I CAN PAY ALL CASH."

Though I admire the spirit of independence in the person who would make such a statement, that attitude is no way to get rich.

There's nothing wrong with debt if it is used prudently. If you're truly worried about foreclosure, then scale back the debt, but don't eliminate it entirely. After all, you should be only getting into deals that generate significant cash flow even *after* debt service. In that case, why wouldn't you want to use other people's money to magnify your own profits, unless perhaps you have a religious aversion to it?

I was on stage a couple of months ago with Nicole, one of my successful students from Maryland. She was describing how she owned 1,100 multi-family units in six different emerging markets across the United States. I asked her what kind of cash flow she was generating, and she said, "Dave, sorry, but that's none of your business—but I will tell you this much: I just a new commercial building for one million dollars and I paid all cash."

She got big applause from the audience, but only a short, polite clap from me! Sure I'm proud of Nicole, but she's missing out on a major opportunity. She can benefit from the profit from one property worth $1 million, or from three to 10 more, all with her same current assets.

Even professional investors are subject to this mistake. I sat on a panel at a big real estate convention in Baltimore along with a guy who bragged that he owned 45 single-family houses with zero debt.

Both he and my student Nicole failed to make one key calculation: return on equity. They both had nice bank balances, but that equity was not working hard enough for them.

$$\text{Return On Equity} = \frac{\text{Cash Flow After Taxes}}{\text{Cash Invested}}$$

Here's another way to put it: Don't impress me by your cash flow. Instead, impress me by how much cash flow you generate compared with how much you invest.

Take Advantage of Several Financing Sources Available to You

It's crucial that you understand that last point about making your money work as hard as you do. Of course, you may not be in a position right now even to consider buying a property with all cash. Let's look at all the options you have for financing your deals.

Local Banks

In this category I'm including commercial banks and savings and loan companies. Even though these are the boring, traditional sources of financing, sometimes they are your best choice. Local lenders like to loan to people and properties right in their area. They're very familiar with property values and in some cases may need less convincing.

Local banks are good to use for repositioning projects. They typically have favorable construction loan terms and like to do business with people they know. If you are investing in areas outside of your home base, I suggest you set up a meeting or lunch with a local lender whenever you are in the area. The better they know you, the higher the probability that you will get the loan.

Local banks tend to have shorter loan terms and slightly higher interest rates, which makes the payments higher on these loans. This means you will be sacrificing cash flow. If you have a deal that is somewhat tight on the numbers, it's worth considering a national lender or conduit lender.

National Lenders

Most of these lenders have very precise lending criteria to judge their loans. That is because they intend not to hold those loans, but to sell them on the *secondary market* very shortly after the loan closes.

The main secondary markets are *Freddie Mac* and *Fannie Mae*. These are government-sponsored—but not government-guaranteed—buyers of loans. These loans usually have the lowest interest rates available.

Conduit Lenders

These are Wall Street firms such as Lehman Brothers and Citigroup. They pool their loans together into buckets (the Wall Street suits like to call them *tranches*), thus creating *mortgage-backed securities*. They then sell them on the open market. The loans tend to have higher interest rates, but are sometimes less conservative with their qualifying criteria.

Other conduit lenders include insurance companies and pension funds. These companies usually only want to lend amounts of several million dollars at a minimum.

Here are some general guidelines: When you need money to rehab a property, consider local banks. Go to national lenders when you have a straightforward *cookie-cutter* deal, and approach conduit lenders when you require the lender to be more creative in its *underwriting* or due diligence process to get you approved.

YOUR MORTGAGE BROKER—MONEY WELL SPENT

Mortgage brokers are to investors what sports agents are to athletes. They're expensive, but you're paying for their vast knowledge and their ability to present you in the best possible light.

Good brokers have a long list of contacts at all three of the types of lenders I mentioned earlier. Not only can they help you to judge whether the deal you're reviewing is a winner, but they'll tell you right away whether it can be financed, and on what terms. This saves you time and money.

Cultivate these people because they also know everyone in town. Need a quick drive-by on a property, or a reference to a good management company or attorney? Your broker will know.

THE MANY TYPES OF LOANS

We just discussed lenders; now let's look at the different types of loans that are available.

Conventional

These are the *garden variety* of loans that are not insured by the federal government. The loan might be *conforming*, meaning that the property and borrower meet all the standards of Fannie Mae and Freddie Mac. There are also plenty of loans done on a non-conforming basis. A *jumbo loan* of more than about $750,000 is one example.

Government

The government has many different loan programs to service a variety of needs. These loans usually have the benefit of low-interest rates, longer loan terms, and low up-front costs. The drawback is that there are usually some operating restrictions tied to the property that is awarded one of these loans. The most common is a rent restriction which states that rents can be no higher than a certain percentage of the market. The ceiling is usually below whatever the market rents are.

Construction

Whenever your property will need repairs greater than three percent of the purchase price, you will probably take out a construction loan.

These are short-term loans, usually between one and three years. They are frequently done on an interest-only basis. Some lenders will conveniently *roll the loan* and make it a conventional loan once construction is completed. If that feature is not available, you may have to refinance out of the construction loan and into a conventional one.

Mezzanine

This is the loan to use when a project needs financing that's greater than 80 percent of property value. Mezzanine financing will not get you to 100 percent of property value, but you might reach 90 percent.

Frequently a first mortgage lender will have a mezzanine program in place to lend you the extra ten percent. Sometimes your broker will find a lender who specializes in mezzanine debt and will provide that extra 10 percent (or more or less) on top of your first mortgage.

Naturally, mezzanine debt carries a higher interest rate than the primary financing. You also must be sure that your primary lender allows mezzanine or *secondary* financing. If it will not allow such a loan, your alternative is to find a primary lender who will.

Bridge

These loans bridge the gap between needing to close now on a property and eventually getting a permanent loan. There may be something about the property that does not conform to underwriting standards, but will conform later.

For instance, you may have a great deal, but occupancy is currently below 85 percent. In order to get a permanent loan at the best long-term interest rate, most lenders require occupancy to be above 85 percent. They call that *stabilized occupancy*.

Your bridge lender will recognize the quality of the deal and the predicament you're in. This lender will be happy to finance the property—for a higher interest rate and with your property as collateral. As soon as you reach 85 percent occupancy, you swap out that loan for the lower-cost, permanent one.

Small Business Administration

You can get insured loans from an SBA-approved lender if you agree to be the majority occupant in the building. You can often get in with a down payment as low as ten percent, and interest rates are usually lower than with a conventional loan.

Private Money

One of my favorite sources is private citizens with money to lend. Their money is just as green as what you find at banks, but without the bureaucratic hoops to jump through.

One subset of private money is *angel investors*. These are high-net-worth individuals who lend between $100,000 and $10 million. We discuss angel investors later in the chapter.

Hard Money

When I first used hard-money lenders, I thought they were perhaps connected with the mob. Maybe it had to do with my first hard-money lender, who insisted on meeting me at the local donut shop. He wore an old, round-brimmed hat and was dressed like a gangster. Maybe it had to do with the rates I was being charged—between 17 and 20 percent, plus another five points! (One point is one percent of the loan amount, paid up front.) Can you blame me for drawing that conclusion?

I then discovered that hard-money lenders are often simply wealthy, honest individuals who've carved out a specialized niche for themselves.

I've just told you the worst aspect of working with these lenders—they cost an arm and a leg. Here's the great aspect: They don't care about you.

In other words, you could be from Mars. If the deal you bring them is good, then your lack of experience, lousy credit rating, or other problems simply don't matter. They'll lend you money on the deal, collateralized by that deal. If you can't pay, they get the deal.

I financed a lot of commercial properties with hard money at the beginning of my career. I discovered that if my deal was good enough, these lenders would give me 100 percent financing, and they would act quickly.

I got into a few properties that generated excellent cash flow. That allowed me to refinance them for much lower rates and pay off the hard-money lenders. Now I had even better cash flow.

I laugh when I hear people slam hard-money lenders, saying that they would never consider paying someone so much interest. By setting arbitrary limits on themselves, they will not benefit from a whole class of deals. These are the deals that don't work with conventional financing, but are so good that they can pay back the hard-money lender, plus provide the investor with a great return.

GETTING THE LOAN APPROVED

Now that we've covered many of your options for getting financed, let's talk about what it takes to get a loan approved.

Just as you did your due diligence on the deal, lenders will go through a similar process. They will check the past two years of profit-and-loss statements, plus the year-to-date one. They'll examine the current rent roll and will inspect the exterior and interior of the property. At first it's just a visual inspection. If they decide to get serious with the deal, they'll send out their own property inspector.

The great thing about commercial real estate is that much of the lending decision rests on the merits of the property and not on you personally. Nevertheless, conventional lenders do pay some attention to the person requesting the loan. Therefore they will want to see your own financial statement. In addition, they'll want a schedule of real estate you own, and will check your credit history.

The next step will be for the lender to send you a *term sheet*. This is between 5 and 30 pages long, explaining the terms of the deal. It indicates whether the deal is *recourse* or *non-recourse*. Recourse means you are personally liable for the debt, and non-recourse means you are not.

Most people naturally prefer non-recourse loans. The tradeoff is that non-recourse financing often comes with burdensome pre-payment penalties. That's okay if you plan to hold the deal for an extended period.

On the other hand, if you plan to sell the property fairly quickly, you should discuss the best options with your mortgage broker.

Insider Tip

Many investors don't realize that the term sheet is negotiable. Even though it comes printed on official letterhead, you don't have to take what they give you. If your deal is good enough (where did we see that point before?) there will be other lenders who would love to do business with you. If there is something in the term sheet that you would like to change, call the lender and start negotiating. If you're not comfortable negotiating the first time out, then have your attorney do it and listen in on the call.

Attorneys who specialize in real estate are well-versed in negotiating term sheets. One key negotiating point is the amount of money that the lender will require up front to start the process. It is likely to be between $7,000 and $25,000. One lender wanted $95,000 from me and I got 'em down to $9,000.

Part of this up-front money is for the costs that lenders incur at this stage. These include reports from the third parties who are doing the appraisal, the environmental study (or studies), and the property inspection. Make sure the lender orders the appraisal as soon as possible, because it can take from four to six weeks to complete. If there is anything that consistently holds up deals, it's that appraisal.

The lender will not start the process until the initial fee is paid and a copy of the purchase and sale agreement, signed by both parties, is submitted. Why? Because it's not a deal until both parties sign the P&S.

Someone at the lender's office now gathers up all these reports from you and the lender's own experts, and sends a package to the lender's underwriting unit. That's where they decide whether to do your deal.

It's at this stage that you can improve your chances immensely. Create your own presentation to the underwriter. Of course you will not be in the room when your deal is formally discussed, nor are you likely to meet the underwriter. That's all the more reason to prepare a package that *can* be in the room, and can do the talking for you.

The goal is to present your deal in such a way that it answers every question that might be in the underwriter's mind, even before it's asked. You do this by presenting an overwhelming amount of information about yourself and the deal.

Here is a list of items that you should submit in your loan package:

- Executive summary
- Appraisal
- Financial statement
- Credit report
- Sponsor financial statement
- Property financials
- Borrower resume
- Purchase and sale agreement
- Legal description of the property
- Photographs
- Map location
- Environmental information
- Property management documents

The executive summary should have all the critical dates of the project spelled out, such as the effective date, due-diligence expiration date, and the closing date. If you are doing a Section 1031 like-kind exchange, add any dates that are critical for that to go smoothly.

If you have an old appraisal on the property, add it to your package. Even though the lender will do its own fresh appraisal, it will appreciate the information on your prior one, such as any comparable properties that the previous appraiser used at the time to determine value.

If your own financial statement is weak, you may consider getting a strong partner for the deal. This person is sometimes called a *sponsor*. You then get to add your sponsor's financial statement to the package.

Put in your resume. This is your opportunity to sell yourself. If you've done any real estate deals in the past, talk about them here. If you have not, then it's appropriate to describe what training or other relevant activities you've been involved in. Remember that everyone started out at some point, so any lack of resume items is not only temporary on your part, but it's natural. You're not the focus of the deal—your strong deal will be.

Do you know people who will say good things about you? Ask them to write you up a character letter. It could even be something unrelated to real estate, such as from a minister or scoutmaster where you volunteered. Do anything you can think of to help sell yourself to the underwriter. This is not the time to be shy.

Your small binder should include all the property financials, nicely organized. Add a signed copy of the purchase and sale agreement along with a legal description of the property.

Put photos of the property in the package, if they help *sell the sizzle*. Get the best angles during the best light of the day. Do not put in pictures of the repairs that must be done to the property. That's the job of the lender's inspector, who will inform the underwriter of any necessary repairs.

Put a map in the package showing where the property is located. The bank will be interested to see what type of street the property is on. Is it a main street with substantial traffic? Is it conveniently located just a short distance from a main artery that would be too busy for easy left-turn access? Try to identify the positive aspects of the location; after all, you should have taken this into consideration during your due diligence phase.

If you have copies of old Phase I or Phase II environmental reports, include them. They will not be current, but could nonetheless help the lender to know when the property was judged to be free from hazards.

Finally, include the property management documents. This is one of the most important parts of the package. The bank will definitely want to know who will be managing the property and the experience level of that manager. If it's your first deal, this is your opportunity to make it clear that *you* won't be the manager!

The management company should provide you with a professionally written resume that talks about their experience and why they are qualified to do the deal. They must also give you a marketing plan to explain their process for filling and maintaining the property. They'll also include one-year and five-year projections for the property. This is great stuff to have in your binder.

You may think that I'm being inconsistent here, suggesting that you include projections when I blasted the use of pro forma numbers in previous chapters. There is no inconsistency. I said you should not base your buying decision on the seller's projections. You definitely should have developed some projections of your own, with the help of your management company. It's simply good business to manage to goals.

The whole idea is to sell yourself and the deal. The underwriting package you create is actually a marketing package that shows your professionalism. The better you anticipate and answer any objection that might be in the lender's mind, the better your chances of getting the deal funded. And believe me—your professional package will be a rare treat for these people. There you go again, being easy to do business with!

ASSUMING THE EXISTING DEBT

Some investors get excited when they hear that the seller's existing loan can be assumed. They think they can just take over the payments and be done with the financing, without lots of paperwork or closing costs.

Times have changed. Now you must be *qualified* by the bank who holds the mortgage. They want to make sure you know what you're doing and can make the payments. They also will charge you one point along the way.

In addition, though the closing costs can be much less than with a new loan, you still must pay certain expenses because you still need to do your due diligence.

You don't always have to cajole a seller into assuming the debt. In fact, sometimes the seller will state in the listing agreement that the loan must be assumed. There may be a hefty pre-payment penalty on the loan and the seller does not want to eat that charge.

If you think you may want to assume a mortgage, here are some points to consider.

In my experience, the assumption process takes a minimum of 90 days to complete. This means that if you sign a contract to close in 60 days, it's not going to happen. You might as well get the 90 days up front because if you later apply for an extension, you may not get it and you would be out-of-pocket for all of your due-diligence costs.

Trust me—it will take 90 days regardless of what the seller says. Often it will take longer. It's smart to build an automatic extension into your purchase and sale agreement. It gets triggered if the lender delays the closing because the assumption process is still going on. I recently closed on one that took five months to complete.

Next, be sure to ask what the prepayment penalty is. You ought to know what it's going to cost you if you assume the loan and for some reason want to pay it off before the prepayment penalty is up.

Of course, ask when that prepayment penalty expires. You may plan on holding the property for three to five years and the prepayment penalty expires in year three. That works.

What if the prepayment penalty is not up for another seven years? Then it's time to ask the next question—will the loan be assumable again by another, future buyer?

Many loans have the ability to be assumed two or three different times; sometimes they can only be assumed once. You must know your options up front.

Of course, one of the most important questions is the interest rate on the loan. If it's a nice low rate—and it's assumable again—it may be attractive to your future buyer.

What if it's higher than market rate? That makes no difference if the property throws off great cash flow. I've had properties generate cash with mortgages at 18 percent!

If you assume the mortgage, be sure to watch those interest rates. Imagine if it's cash flowing now, and interest rates are favorable when the prepayment penalty burns off. You can hold the property, refinance it, and watch your cash flow soar.

There's Plenty of Room for Creativity

You might very well get your deal funded through conventional lenders, especially if you provide that professional loan package. But what if the usual lenders say "no," for whatever reason?

Don't despair, because a great many commercial properties are financed using imaginative approaches. I mentioned some of these earlier, but they're important to cover again.

It's common to negotiate seller financing on deals, but the specific terms can vary widely. You can pay all of the principal sometime out in the future and not offer the seller any interest whatsoever. As odd as that offer may sound, sellers sometimes agree to it.

You can offer the seller an interest rate but no current payment. Instead all interest will be paid when the loan *matures* or ends. This is good because it does not cut into your cash flow. Or you might structure simple interest payments to be paid monthly. You could *up your offer* with principal and interest payments to be paid monthly.

Don't forget that the seller can even give you the first mortgage for the property, and not only a second. Perhaps the seller would like a monthly annuity, but doesn't want the hassles of management. Carrying a first mortgage, or *taking back paper*, as it's called, would allow the seller to achieve this goal.

You could do a wraparound mortgage. With this approach, you pay the seller one lump sum to cover both the existing first mortgage and the second mortgage. This allows the seller to account for the payment of the first mortgage, so that if you did not make payments, the seller could get the property back.

It's possible to transfer IRA, Keogh, Roth, and SEP money into a true self-directed IRA and invest that money into real estate. You may or may not have significant funds in those vehicles, but there are plenty of people who do in your town! This is one of the great untapped sources of real estate financing in America.

I'm just scraping the surface of the creative options available to you. Want to guess how to find out which approach will work best for your property? That's right—work with your mortgage broker, who eats and sleeps creative loan terms.

Master Lease Options

This is a good option for sellers who will not or cannot sell their property for a variety of reasons. The seller may have a high prepayment penalty that prohibits a sale for another year or two. In this case, the seller could lease the entire property to you in return for a monthly payment. You run the property, collect rents, and pay operating expenses. It may include the option for you to buy the property at a future date at a pre-negotiated price.

Imagine that you increase the value of the property through higher net operating income while you're running the property. At the end of the lease period, you buy the property at a lower price and it is instantly worth more, because you've added value during the lease.

Another reason to arrange a master lease option is if you couldn't get a loan because of lack of experience. The master lease option allows you to run the property for a couple of years and then go back to the bank with a successful track record in hand.

Straight Option

This simply gives you the right to buy the property within a certain period. Donald Trump made millions of dollars with his options on the railroad yards in New York City. He bought the option and waited until the time was right to develop the property. There was a good chance the deal could not be done. If that happened, he would be under no obligation to buy the land. An option that is not exercised only costs the purchaser of the option the amount of the option fee.

That fee can range from a few dollars to $1 million or more, depending on the magnitude of the deal.

Blanket Mortgages

Sometimes lenders or sellers will allow you to have 100 percent financing, or close to it, but require that you put up additional collateral. This is called a *blanket mortgage*. You wrap other properties in the same mortgage for the benefit of the lender. If you default on the primary property, the lender gets all the properties.

Avoid doing this if you possibly can. That's just too much risk for you to take in most situations. Not only might you lose big if something happens, but you've now *encumbered* your other properties. Even if things work out well with the new property, you may find it difficult to resell or refinance the collateral properties when you want to.

Private Money

This is my very favorite financing method. I've already mentioned it briefly, but let's talk more about two forms of private money—equity partnerships and debt partnerships.

When you structure a private-money equity partnership, your job is to bring the deal to the table. Your partner finances the down payment and closing costs. You split the cash flow and profits.

Sometimes the split is 50-50, but it could be 60-40 or 30-70. You do what you must to make the deal appealing, without giving away the farm. In my book, it's better to have only 25 percent of a $10 million deal than it is to have 100 percent of no deal.

When you have multiple partners, it's called a *syndication*. There are a number of very specific rules you must follow to syndicate deals. That's because you most likely will have created a security with your syndication, and now the boys down at the Securities and Exchange Commission will take an interest in what you're doing. And they have no sense of humor.

Equity partnerships are the fastest way to fund your deals because partners get an attractive chunk of any profit for investing their money. Another benefit to you is that because they are equity partners, there's no obligation of a return to them, as there is with debt.

In a debt partnership, investors lend you money in exchange for a good interest rate. Debt partnerships are the cheapest way to fund your deals. You don't give up a chunk of equity, but it will take you longer to raise the funds. In addition, that debt must be paid off before you or any equity partners share in the profits.

HOW TO DEAL WITH INVESTORS

I've raised tens of millions of dollars to fund my real estate deals. Along the way I've discovered two key principles: Constantly communicate with your investors, and be conservative with your projections.

When investors don't hear from you, their imaginations will fill that vacuum, and it won't be with positive images. Communicate with them at least monthly in writing or on a conference call.

Even if you don't have good news to share, keep them current about their investment. Part of your responsibility is to educate them about the *ups and downs* of the deal. When they're regularly informed and have an opportunity to ask questions, they'll be far more patient when times are bad, and delighted when times are good.

Always be conservative with your numbers. The last thing you need is to be stressed-out all the time about hitting your numbers. You're much better off attracting fewer investors but exceeding their expectations. Besides, disgruntled investors have a way of hiring attorneys to get them out of what they consider to be under-performing deals. It would be a shame if your deal was doing okay, but your lofty initial projections led investors to be disappointed nonetheless.

Handle investors correctly and they'll not only want to invest in deal after deal with you, but they'll brag to their rich friends about their great investments with you. Pretty soon you'll have a waiting list of people with money in hand, ready to lend to you. How great is that!

WHERE TO FIND PRIVATE MONEY

Here's the good news: The majority of private money typically comes from friends and family members. Here's the bad news: If you are not careful, money from friends and family can complicate your life.

It's true that these people may know and trust you like no one else can. Unfortunately, sometimes they also carry a lot of memory baggage that drags you down.

For example, today when I meet someone new, I'm known as Dave Lindahl the investor, speaker, and author. But when I happen to meet an old high school buddy at the store, he remembers Dave, the kid who played in a rock band. Family members can be even worse, fixating on ancient history, such as "David, the kid who always threw my newspaper in my flower bed."

If you're blessed with unconditionally positive relatives and close friends, by all means tell them about your real estate investing opportunities. But even then, only tell them once. Do not become a pest, or you will earn comments along the lines of "Uh oh, here comes Dave, wanting us to invest in another one of his deals."

I personally found it easier to get money from my local real estate investment group. These people understood the real estate part of me better. They were going where I wanted to go. Even better, some of them had already been there and could mentor me during the process.

I discovered that there were many people at these meetings who wanted to get into deals, but somehow never could generate a deal on their own. They had money but they didn't have deals.

I would go up in front of the group, tell them about my deal, and ask them to meet me in the back if they were interested in being my partner. This worked very well.

In addition to other investors, you should look at your circle of acquaintances in a new light—your doctor, dentist, attorney, buddies at the gym, and so on.

The trick here is to craft a compelling, quick, and non-pushy statement about what you currently are working on. Then you weave a sentence or two of this statement into your conversation.

I'm not talking about *pitching* these people on your deal. Instead, if in the course of your activities you casually mention that you've been super-busy recently, putting together the financing on the North Point Shopping Center, you can then gauge their reaction.

If you see zero response, then you might drop the subject. You're more likely to hear "Oh? I didn't know you were involved with that property . . ." That gives you a tiny opening to respond "Oh, yeah, I'm assembling a group of investors who could get a nice return. Do you know anyone who might be interested?"

I teach a number of ways to break the ice about your investments in a casual and effective manner. But the point I'm making here is that you'll never know about these potential investment partners if you never ask. And discovering the casual way to raise the subject makes the process stress-free, natural, and highly effective.

Another skill you should develop is to become visible where these potential investors congregate. For instance, business owners often have some money to invest, and they attend meetings at the Chamber of Commerce or Rotary Club. Join organizations like these.

Charitable organizations are filled with local *movers and shakers*. They're the people who regularly donate their money and time. When you donate some of your own time, you become one of them. It's a very wise investment, and you're *doing good* at the same time that you'll be *doing well*.

Angel Investors

The most important private money investor is the *angel investor*. These people are experienced investors with lots of money. They also know many other angel investors, so once you crack open this network, you could potentially be flooded with money.

If you saw some angel investors on the street, you'd never suspect their resources. That's often the case with really wealthy people—they drive plain cars and live in modest homes. It's simply that their bank accounts have inordinate numbers of zeros in them.

Angel investor groups meet regularly in most major cities. Start with Google to find them, and start going to their meetings. They're looking for great opportunities and you need funding, so it's a two-way street.

Your comprehensive loan presentation will come in handy here, in addition to your business plan. The latter should describe where you are planning to go with your business, and not just focus on the one property. It also tells angel investors that you actually sat down and thought it all out, which most people don't do.

Important tip: Your loan presentation may be all that you need to get one investor in your deal, but not to form a syndication. As I stated earlier, there are complex rules to follow when pooling investors' funds. You simply must discuss your syndication intentions with an attorney who specializes in securities law—not real estate law, but securities law.

Want a handy rule of thumb, based on my experience with private money? Of the people who say they will give you money, only about 50 percent will do so. About 20 percent of that 50 percent will back out just before the closing. It's important that you know that sometimes an early "yes" doesn't really turn out to be a "yes."

Therefore, line up more investors than you need, and somewhat oversubscribe your deals. Let investors know that it is *first-come, first-served*, and that you will fill your deal in the order in which you actually receive funds. Anyone who is too slow to act will need to wait until the next deal. The prospect of being left out will result in more investors following through.

The Pros and Cons of Deal Structures

I'm not an attorney and have no plans to become one. Therefore, the following is not legal advice, but instead is my take on the practical aspects of the deal structure you choose.

Attorneys have invented many formats for getting multiple investors into one project. Two common ones are the *tenant-in-common* *(TIC)* entity and the *limited liability company partnership* *(LLC partnership)*.

In a TIC, all investors are considered equal, individual owners of the property. All decisions are discussed among the owners, and no single person controls the deal. In fact, some decisions such as to sell or refinance must be made unanimously.

There is a certain clean, straightforward aspect to TIC ownership, especially if the individuals are all experienced investors. On the other hand, if a TIC-owned property needs additional financing through a traditional lender, the process can be difficult. Each investor must be checked out financially and everyone must sign the closing documents.

The more TIC members you have, the more difficult it is to get the deal done.

I like using the LLC partnership because this allows you to have great control over the deal. There is one chief, and it's you. There is one primary decision maker, and it's you, regardless of the number of partners. You only rarely need to ask partners to vote on matters, and even then it's not a unanimous vote but a simple majority.

I do not mean to imply that you should ignore your partners. I'm simply pointing out that when you are considering *Plan A* and *Plan B*, and investors seem split on which path to take, you get to make the decision.

This type of structure can make your life much easier. You can thank me after your first couple of deals.

In the Next Chapter

We've been diving into the details a lot recently. It's time yet again to have a change of pace and look at the big picture.

In the next chapter I present principles that are potentially worth millions to you, if you choose to do lots of commercial real estate deals.

THE ART OF RAISING MONEY

Raising money, whether it's derived from investors, family, friends, or borrowed from commercial lenders, is one of the most crucial elements in any real estate transaction. The use of borrowed money to buy real estate serves several purposes: It gives you more leverage, which enables you to purchase much more, often 20 or 30 times more than what could otherwise be bought for cash; it reduces your equity exposure; and the interest payments on the loan provide a significant tax deduction.

When Trump invests in a real estate project, he typically puts up less of his own money than you might think. For example, he will often erect a building to either rent out the available space or sell the residential units in it. Typically, his investors in the project will put up 85 percent while Trump puts up 15 percent.

Working with monied outside investors enables Trump to participate in many transactions without monster exposure of dollars in a particular development.

From *Trump Strategies for Real Estate: Billionaire Lessons for the Small Investor*, by George H. Ross (John Wiley & Sons, 2005, page 127).

9

I Wish Someone Had
Told Me These Things

I don't know how old you are, so it's possible that you've never been to a movie with an intermission. *Gone With the Wind* had one. During an intermission, you would get up, stretch, and freshen up before sitting down to finish the movie. Well, we're taking a small intermission now, because you look like you need it.

I've been grinding a lot of information into your head about the precise steps you should take to invest in commercial real estate the smart way. Sometimes it's possible to get so far into the details that you lose track of some of the big-picture principles.

In this chapter I want to take you through a journey of some of the lessons I have learned from many hundreds of real estate deals. I discovered some of them in the nick of time. Others I learned the hard way, and they cost me a great deal of money—in fact, more than a four-year Ivy League education. You get them handed to you, you lucky dog.

WHICH IS MORE IMPORTANT TO YOU: EGO OR MONEY?

I shake my head when I see investors surrounding themselves with a so-called *Dream Team* of people who are not very bright at all. It's not that the investor is cheap; it's that he wants to feel like the smartest person on the team. That's not smart, it's dumb, and it will cost the investor money over time.

You must continually look for the very smartest people you can to aid you in your real estate journey. They cost more, but in another sense, they're free. They will save you and make you much more money than the *bargain-basement* dullards.

It takes a strong personality to be okay with surrounding yourself with people who can do things that you cannot. It's a characteristic of leaders.

You have your function, which is to be the director of the entire production. Your team members all have their functions, too, and they *better* be more knowledgeable than you, or one of you is unnecessary!

When you have the choice of buying a big hot tub or plowing some of that money back into getting better team members, get better team members. Soon they will make you enough money for a hot tub in every room.

START, STUMBLE, AND SUCCEED

Most people have highly active imaginations. They don't just re-live experiences, they *prelive* them. They're able to conjure up multiple disasters if they start a new activity—so they don't start.

It's far more profitable to start and stumble. But do know that you will stumble at first. I've found that very few things truly require us to be perfectly right the first time around. Real estate is not one of them.

The process of buying commercial real estate gives you ample opportunities to *pull off the road and check your directions*. You can ask advisers before you sign anything. Even after you sign, your deposit is refundable until you and your advisors have thoroughly reviewed the deal. Even if you miss a deadline, you often can renegotiate it and still come out okay.

Look at it this way: You're taking a far bigger risk with your financial future by wringing your hands and doing nothing, than you are by starting, stumbling, and eventually succeeding. I believe in my bones that the more action you take, the luckier you get.

Discomfort Breeds Dollars

Are you an introvert? Glad to meet you. So am I, at heart.

I'd much rather be by myself for long stretches of time than fly around the country and get on stage in front of tens of thousands of people.

In one sense, you and I have been fed a pack of lies. We've been told "Do what you love, and you'll be successful." What baloney. Anyone who knows me well is aware that I have a very serious soft spot for chocolate. So I can sit on my duff, eat chocolate, and succeed?

A more accurate way to guide people is to say, "Take action, get results, and you'll be successful." That's not nearly as poetic as the "Do what you love" stuff, but much more truthful.

I suggest that you make it a goal to do something that is out of your comfort zone on a regular basis. Meaning *daily*. Try making an extra offer this week; try going to the Chamber of Commerce cocktail hour and telling three new people what you do; try standing up in front of your local real estate investing association and describing the kind of deal you're looking for.

The key word above is *try*. Draw a circle around your capabilities as of today. Then tomorrow, you should be able to draw a somewhat larger circle. You're getting stronger, better, more knowledgeable, and bolder, while your competition is sitting still, waiting for that *perfect time* which never comes.

Live Where You Want, But Invest Where It Makes Sense

You probably did not make a scientific study before choosing where you live. It might be the hometown you grew up in. Maybe you went to college and stayed in the area. Perhaps you moved where your spouse was given a great job offer.

Those may all be good reasons to live there, but they're not good reasons to invest in those markets. Don't get me wrong: I bought plenty of real estate close to where I lived, for two reasons. First, I didn't know any better. Second, I happened to buy into the market at just the right phase of the cycle for the type of real estate I wanted to buy.

Let me be clear about what I mean when I say *bought into the market at just the right time*: It was a great time, because people universally told me that I was crazy, I would lose my shirt, I should wait until the market firmed up, they had tried real estate and it doesn't work, and so on.

Therefore, if your local market happens to be at the right phase of the cycle for the property type you're buying, go get 'em! If it is not at the right phase, *go find a market that is*.

I spend some time elsewhere in this book discussing how to invest by trusting your instruments and not your eyes. It's comforting to drive by your property every day, but it's much more profitable to invest in a soon-to-explode market. Are you in this business to be comfy or to be rich? Have your property manager do the heavy lifting at your property.

A Real Litmus Test of Quality

If your management company cannot provide you with frequent reports on all aspects of your property, it's not a good management company.

They must have their act together to provide frequent reports. They need to have systematized their business. That involves understanding it in the first place, then documenting those systems and having the people and tools necessary to get the reports out on time. Those are all characteristics of solid companies in any industry. When one or more of those parts is missing, you get excuses instead of reports: "Our guy was sick today, so that's why they're late," or "We're training a new person to get the reports out." All fine and dandy . . . for some other investor to endure. You, on the other hand, should only go with the outfit that delivers all the reports on time, period.

It's interesting that this same litmus test applies to property sellers, too: If you have to beg and cajole the seller to deliver various documents during the due-diligence phase, the chances are, oh, 95 percent or better that you're dealing with a substandard property. The only exception I can think of is when someone inherits a property and is trying to sell it off. That person may not know a thing about the property, or even who has the information about it. I'm good with that—as long as I'm getting a fantastic price, I'm willing to be patient in those circumstances.

The Three Things You Cannot Delegate

If you want to grow your real estate investing business, you must continually look for ways to delegate. I spoke at length about this in an earlier chapter. As soon as you understand something and it's systematized, off it should go to someone who can help you get it done.

If you don't understand something—such as real estate law—you must, of course, delegate those tasks. At first, when money is short, you must be creative about using lower-cost help for some tasks. Then, after just one or two deals, you can and should be delegating like crazy.

The danger comes after the fifth, tenth, or twentieth deal: You get good at delegating at the same time that you get lazy.

First, you decide to hire someone to do your marketing. Later, you hand off the financing relationships to someone, because you have the dough to do it. You decide that you're almost done, and then delegate the last remaining big responsibility, which is to manage the managers.

You're almost done, all right. Your company will now grind to a halt, or worse, die. You cannot delegate the marketing, financing, and managing aspects. I'm not saying you must do every aspect of them yourself. By all means hire people to assemble and distribute the marketing materials, schedule meetings with brokers and private money lenders, and prepare property management reports.

You must stay on top of these areas, though, because they're your highest and best use. If you continuously perform these duties, you can reproduce your success anywhere in the country. If you *set them and forget them*, like some expensive alarm clock, you're going to have a rude awakening when your company gets away from you and deals grind to a halt.

REPUTATION TRUMPS REVENUES

In this ultrawired world, news travels fast. Even so, real estate investors love to engage in a practice that is thousands of years old—they gossip.

When you make news by being a great guy or a jerk, you can be sure that the real estate community knows about it within days. I was surprised to find out how small the commercial real estate investing world really is. After you have played the game for only a little while, you will realize that you know almost all of the players at your level and at the next level above. As you increase the size of your portfolio, this principle will still hold true.

The way you do deals and manage properties will soon be reduced to sound bytes and labels:

- "She's a straight-shooter."
- "When he says he'll do it, it's as good as done."

- "Add fifty percent to any deadline this guy promises you, because he will *not* be on time."
- "Go ahead and do the deal, but remember that the deal that just bombed on the South Side was also his."

I caution you elsewhere in this book to make sure that the person you're negotiating with also gets a good deal. If your ego insists that you act like the Terminator in every transaction, your movie career will soon be over.

When in doubt, think about what will most burnish your reputation for the long term, and take that option. When the next sweet, off-market deal comes along, the other party will often choose the investor with the best reputation.

Pay Them Fast

Years ago I started a contracting business. Sometimes I had 18 guys and up to 30 sub-contractors doing business for me on multiple projects.

I was given a simple but great piece of advice by my mentor, Mark Shavel: *Always pay your subcontractors fast.* When they call to get a check, show up at the job site with checkbook in hand. If they complete the job properly, cut the check on the spot.

Yes, the contract stipulates that I have three days to inspect and another seven days to cut the check. Other, so-called *clever*, contractors would push this delay to the limit. Mark said that if I paid faster than expected, I'd be the favorite contractor, and was he ever right.

Really good subcontractors are hard to find and harder to keep because they are in such high demand. By being known as a good and fast payer, these *subs*, as they were known, were eager to work for me. In fact, they were willing to drop what they were doing when I had an emergency or needed a particular job done really fast.

Here, too, word would get around that "Lindahl's a good guy to work for." That seven-word testimonial was precious to me, and made my projects go so much better.

Don't Confuse Distraction with Diversification

I've talked about the people who never get around to taking action. Let's now discuss the people who take too much action.

On the face of it, they should be the superachievers, right? Not so. Their problem is that they flit from one idea, deal, and market to the next, and never really get good at anything.

It's great to be enthusiastic about all the possibilities you see. The only way to capitalize on them is to make a decision about which is the best to do first, and then to do it to the best of your ability.

Decide and do. Don't *dream and dabble.* As you gain experience and resources, you may be able to increase your capacity and do several projects in multiple markets simultaneously.

When you're that good, you'll still have an appetite that's larger than what you can effectively complete. Believe me, it's sometimes painfully difficult to fly into a market, see a tremendous amount of opportunity, and have the self-discipline to say to yourself, "Not now."

Pick up a book called *Flow*, by Mihaly Csikszentmihalyi. Some name, huh? But it's a great book. He talks about how to find that *sweet spot* in which you do your best work. He explains that if your work is too easy, you get bored and disengage, but if your work is too hard, you get frustrated and disengage.

Perhaps you will not find much success in a given market because you misread the phase that it's in. It's fine to move on to another market or type of commercial deal. Just be honest with yourself first: Are you moving on after having given it a very solid try, or are you bailing out? Your conscience will know.

These Eight Words Tell Me Everything

"How many offers did you make last week?"

That's it. That's all I have to ask another investor in order to get a pretty good idea of that person's business.

When you are starting out, you should be making at least two offers a week. This is what I require my coaching students to do. But what if there are no decent properties to make an offer on? Then you make an offer based on the current numbers. Explain to the seller or broker why you're making such a low-ball offer, and ask if you should still submit it. I mentioned this technique earlier, and how you will occasionally be told, "Okay, send it to me."

Even if that does not happen, you've accomplished something—you took action and proposed a transaction. Offer by offer, you will get better at analyzing deals, presenting your terms, negotiating, and reading the other person. You're turning into a professional.

Two offers a week. People often ask me: "What's a good offer-to-acceptance ratio?" That's going to differ throughout your career.

At the beginning, you'll do very few of the deals you make offers on. You have yet to establish your relationships, and many of the deals you'll first be exposed to are not very good. Then your relationships start kicking in—if you follow my advice in this book. You begin to build rapport and establish your reputation as a closer, and the choice deals begin to come your way.

Your ratio will drop from 1 in 20 to 1 in 3. You will only chase after good deals where the seller is willing to give you actual financials so you can make an educated offer.

Strange as it may seem, the way to get to that great 1-in-3 ratio is not to be highly selective with your offers at first, but to just get out there and do them again and again.

GIVE BEFORE YOU GET

I own a real estate brokerage company. When I started it, I did what you are doing right now—I acquired as much knowledge as I could, so I wouldn't have to learn it all through trial-and-error-and-more-error.

I came across Floyd Wickman, who specialized in real estate brokerage. Floyd had the best scripts in the business. I listened and engrained those scripts first in my head, then in the heads of all my agents. Those tools made us hundreds of thousands of dollars.

Floyd had a motto: "We get by giving." He even had lapel pins made up with that saying. I've always remembered that, because his simple statement has made me a fortune over the years.

Call it *karma*, call it the *law of reciprocity*, call it whatever you want, but it works.

Look around and satisfy a need that someone has, and you will be repaid in spades. Make it a habit to be a *net giver* and you can't help but benefit. Go the extra mile to get a transaction completed for a broker or seller and you will get something in return; maybe not right away, but definitely in the future.

I'm not talking about mysticism or religion here. You can be cold and calculating if you choose; but if you first give something of genuine value, it has a way of ricocheting around and eventually coming back to you. I can't explain it—I just know that it works, and hope you try it.

TAME THE OVERACTIVE SPREADSHEET

Many investors spend time making sure they get the expenses right while analyzing a deal, and also assume that the value of the property will increase. Big mistake. This is not looking at the deal through the eyes of a conservative investor, but through the eyes of a speculator.

I've seen spreadsheets that are even worse—they not only show increasing property values, but they increase that value faster than they escalate costs. You can take a pastrami-on-rye and make it look like a phenomenal deal if you aggressively model it in a spreadsheet.

Don't get caught up in the hype, regardless of what an anxious broker or seller is promising.

If you want to be a conservative investor, you must assume three things:

1. The project will take longer than you thought.

2. It will cost more than you thought.
3. When the time comes to resell the property, it will be at the current after-repaired market value.

This is a solid formula for success.

Loyalty Begets Loyalty

One of the qualities I admire and seek out from other people is loyalty. Very few people with this quality will come into your life. When you find someone who does, latch onto this person and be just as loyal in return.

There is no better feeling than knowing you can trust another person. Trust is not given, but is earned through performance. Trust and loyalty go hand in hand. When you build a team of people around you who respect you as much as you respect them, you will truly have built a solid foundation on which you can conduct your business and your life.

In order to get loyalty, you've got to give it. Sometimes you must make hard choices to stay loyal to those who are loyal to you. It may even not be in your short-term best interests to be loyal, but I maintain that it usually is for the long term. This is the true test of loyalty.

Nothing in your business can substitute for loyal team members. I know some commercial real estate companies that are constantly in a state of chaos. The owner shows zero loyalty to his associates. He bases every decision purely in his immediate best interest. Because of that, he has a high associate turnover.

I know another woman with a similar company. Every time you call her office, somebody new answers the telephone, because almost everyone soon quits or is fired. Her life is in a constant state of turmoil, mostly due to her inability to treat people properly.

I'm fortunate to have come across a group of people who share the same primary business values. As soon as they realize that one member needs help, they spring into action, well before being asked. I suggest you spend some time assembling a team that has a similar chemistry. It will make your daily activities immeasurably more pleasant and profitable.

CHARACTER TRAITS

Be coachable. A great many successful people have a coach or mentor. These may be formal or informal arrangements, but they're critical to your success. Someone has already been down the road you seek to travel. Not only can mentors help you to clear any obstacles, but they hold you accountable.

On second thought, that's not quite true. In reality, it's your self-esteem that holds you accountable to the mentor, after you commit to something. Continuously be on the lookout for these people. The good ones can save you literally years of dead ends.

Be decisive. When a window of opportunity opens, pass through it, even if you haven't entirely mapped out what's on the other side. Unsuccessful people spend their time wondering if it's the right time to pass through and second-guessing themselves until it's too late.

If you want to be successful, decide and go forward. You will be rewarded more than you mess up. If you are perpetually indecisive, someday you'll look back and lament "I should have, I could have. . . ."

Practice creative discipline toward your goals. Life constantly gets in the way of your goals. The great commander, Hannibal, marched war elephants through the mountain passes to Italy more than 2,000 years ago, declaring: "We shall either find a way, or make one." That attitude will not only make you famous, it will make you rich.

IN THE NEXT CHAPTER

I trust you're refreshed from our intermission? We now move on to the final elements involved in getting your first commercial real estate deal done.

Any way you look at it, commercial real estate is a complex undertaking. It's a good thing that you don't have to do it all yourself. The next chapter is all about the team of skilled specialists you should assemble to help make you rich.

 DON'T GET TOO COMFORTABLE

It's easy to take the conventional route and not make waves, but the easiest way can be the mediocre way; it may be little more than just treading water. That's okay if you're content with being comfortable and avoiding challenges, but it's not what I want from life.

When you begin feeling comfortable, it should sound an alarm that alerts you that you might be falling into a trap. Ask yourself "Have I stopped moving or have I become stuck?"

From *Trump University: Real Estate 101*, John Wiley & Sons, 2006, 82.

10

YOU'LL NEVER GET
RICH BY YOURSELF

 AMATEUR MISTAKE: "IF I WANT IT DONE RIGHT, I NEED TO DO IT MYSELF."

I don't know who first said this, but I can tell you that it was not someone who became rich.

Let's get something out of the way right up front: You probably can do a few things better than most people. You may even be able to do one or two things better than just about anyone.

So what. If you are serious about becoming *seriously* rich, then you must get beyond your own skills, because you need a whole variety of talents. And you can't possibly be superior at all of them.

You must now acquire a new skill—the ability to change your attitude about delegation.

First, recognize that for many tasks, perfection is wasteful. It's the 80/20 Principle at work again: If you want to go for perfection, you'll spend 80 percent of your time on just that last 20 percent of improvement. I'm here to tell you that it's usually not worth it.

Know when to stop. Demand high-quality work from yourself and the people with whom you work, but also know when to say it's *good enough*. For instance, you won't make extra money by scouring your market for 25 comparable properties, when 10 is more than sufficient.

Amateur Mistake (*Continued*)

You will not close a better deal by running 100 scenarios in your financial model when a half dozen should give you all the information you need.

Your goal must not be simply to *get it done right,* but instead it should be to *get lots of good work done quickly.*

I can judge the future success of investors by another characteristic: They take action before they're 100 percent ready. In practice that means they are impatient to succeed, so they delegate before they're rich.

I realize you may be short on funds to delegate much. I have two responses for that: First, we discussed in earlier chapters how you should be focusing on deals that are so good, they can help to support your team of specialists. If you manage the negotiations the way I suggested, you may be funding your mortgage broker and attorney from the proceeds of the deal.

Second, you must get creative about delegation. Find no-cost helpers like family members and good friends, whom you will remember when the dough starts rolling in. Find low-cost helpers at senior citizen centers, VFW halls, high schools, and so on. They can help to get your marketing materials out into the community, run errands, and screen phone calls, among other tasks.

Of course you can have a hand-picked crack team of assistants surrounding you someday, but that's after you take these initial steps to delegate right away, even though you could do those tasks yourself.

Your *highest and best use* is to be a rainmaker. It's you who brings in the business. Your role is to cultivate key relationships and watch them grow into money trees. As long as you're focused on doing that—and not a thousand details—your business will be successful.

Now that I have mercilessly beat this principle into your head, let's look at other traits that successful businesses share.

The Three Things That All Good Businesses Do

There are simply too many moving parts in business to keep things *steady*, *just so*, or *as-is*. Therefore, your business is either growing, or it's in decline.

Create New Channels

Your business will grow when you create new channels for business to flow to you. The way you do that is by building relationships and improving your marketing methods.

Let's say you decide to increase your business by starting a new marketing channel. You'll do direct mail campaigns to owners who have owned their properties for 20 years or more. These people may be ready to retire or may have depreciated their assets to the point that they're looking to replace them.

You send out a batch of letters and get a few sellers to call. So far so good, but this is where people often make a mistake: They stop their marketing in order to work the deal. One of two things will then happen.

Best case: They move ahead with the deal and perhaps 90 days later they have a cashier's check for a nice amount—but their marketing engine is stone-cold with no new leads coming in.

Worst case: The deal falls through, there is no cashier's check to celebrate over, and their marketing engine is stone-cold.

Either way, you're hurting yourself. You must walk and chew gum. You must be working on your deal at the same time you're keeping that new source of deals humming along. Can you do it all by yourself? Probably not. That's why you must delegate as many parts of it as you can.

Create New Streams of Cash

Cash flow is king in almost any business. The lack of cash flow is the number one reason that businesses die.

When in doubt, opt for the avenue that gives you more cash flow. I've done hundreds of single-family deals in my career, but I much prefer commercial properties because they lubricate my business with large amounts of fresh cash on a monthly basis.

When my mortgage broker presents me with a couple of financing opportunities on a deal, I'll usually take the one that requires less of my cash, even if it means somewhat less ultimate profit.

When investing in a commercial property, you increase cash flow mainly through your selection of the right property management company. Your manager in turn increases cash flow by raising rents, marketing the property effectively in order to increase occupancy, and all the other activities aimed at keeping happy, paying tenants at your property.

Your manager is of course central to the expense-control side of the equation, too. For instance, by jumping on maintenance issues instead of ignoring them, they are guarding your cash.

Cash Checks

This is the fun part, and it's why we're in business. When you've been investing for a while, you can afford to have less-frequent but bigger paydays. I recommend that early on, you try to arrange a series of smaller checks that come in regularly. By *small*, I mean they can still be nice, five-figure or maybe six-figure checks. Just make sure you're seeing them regularly. That way, your brain will closely connect the reward with all the effort you're expending to learn the business, delegate, negotiate, and be creative in a hundred different ways.

YOUR SKILL MULTIPLIERS

In an earlier chapter I discussed how you can get *money multipliers* into your life. Instead of being limited by your own funds, you can use conventional and unconventional lenders to provide all the money you need to finance your deals.

You'll give another major boost to your investing career when you assemble a team of specialists. They are your *skill multipliers*.

In the *bad old days*, you could go to a village doctor who knew everything there was to know about medicine. His prescriptions involved incantations, bloodletting, and perhaps a leech or two. Today, if an eye doctor helped with your difficult pregnancy, it would be cause for a lawsuit.

Real estate is no different. The field has exploded in terms of complexity. Not only does each state have its own rules, but there is a huge variety of financing options. Property management firms also can be highly specialized for a particular property type. There's even an entire industry of shopping specialists who can tell you precisely where to place store displays for maximum visibility and sales.

You don't need to hire an army at first; just start the process. Once you do, and you see the power and effectiveness that it brings to your investing, you won't go back.

Many deals are puzzles. Why labor over them, sweating about whether you're missing or misinterpreting something, when you can simply pick up the phone and find out? An expert has been down that road many times before and can tell you in 60 seconds what to do. That crumb of information could spare you some losses or make you a hundred thousand dollars.

Your Home Team

Let's look at the core of your team—your *home team*—the people you should begin to cultivate immediately.

The Assistant

This person will work side-by-side with you in your office or be available on a moment's notice. He will be the most important person you add to your team early in your career.

I have a prediction: Before you get an assistant you'll not know how you will fill that person's time, nor how you will afford him. After you get an assistant, you'll kick yourself for not getting one sooner. That's because you will not believe how fast your business grows after you get that person.

Don't believe me? Then it's time for you to do a time audit. You should take a solid week and mark down everything you do in your waking hours. Just fold up a sheet of paper in your pocket and put down a series of simple rows that give the ending time, minutes since your last entry, and activity.

One entry might read: *9:14 A.M. 14. Read newspaper.*

The next entry will be: *9:40 A.M. 26. On* loopnet.com *looking for deals.*

The first day or two, you'll forget to write down much of your day. But stick with it! You simply must know exactly where your time goes over the course of a week. Do not be selective in putting down only the high-payoff activities. We're looking for the low ones, too. Also do not cheat and try to remember at the end of the day what you did. It simply will not be accurate.

I think I know what you'll discover: You will spend a small amount of time on things that only you can and should do—talking with the mortgage broker, writing up an offer, or solving a vexing problem. You will be depressed when you identify a large group of activities that someone else could do, even if not quite as well as you can.

That's what you need to delegate as soon as possible to this person. After I got my first assistant, my business soared. I had free time to do more marketing, see more properties, and create more relationships. Because now I could do more rainmaking tasks—which I loved to do—I was on an upward spiral of growing my business and creating more streams of monthly cash.

You don't need to hire a *headhunter* to find these people. First get the word out among people you know that you need a part-time or full-time person. Also consider putting a notice on craigslist.com, which is a great community bulletin board.

The Marketer

The second person I put on my home team would stuff and stamp envelopes for me so that I could get them out to motivated sellers.

When this person came on my team, I finally had a constant flow of letters going out the door weekly. Soon my phone rang consistently.

I was now talking to more sellers, looking at more properties, making more offers, and closing more deals.

I also loved the fact that once I built this minisystem and put it into motion, it worked with very little involvement by me.

As your activities grow, you'll add bookkeeping talent. Of course, you may find one person with several skills that you need, so this becomes your go-to person for quite some time. Then consider hiring someone under your assistant. That way, you're not multiplying your managing workload, and still have only one *direct report*. Plus, your assistant now has increased status and the newly hired person will begin to see a career path.

One of the best uses of your time will be to challenge yourself to see just how much you can delegate and still monitor effectively. When you get good at this, you will not believe how it contributes not only to your success, but to your peace of mind.

Your Deal Team

After your home team begins to take shape, begin to build your *deal team*. These people will help to bring you deals, analyze them, and make them happen.

Brokers

You already know my opinion of these people. They are your secret weapon to real estate riches—*if* you cultivate them carefully and professionally.

Cultivate relationships with as many brokers in each of your target markets as you can. Diversify your relationships, just as brokers would never dream of relying on a single buyer for their deals.

In Chapter Three I discussed how to stand out from other investors when dealing with brokers. When you find yourself thinking, *Man, I'm putting a lot of time into cultivating this broker,* also remember that this person may be capable of handing you a deal worth a year's salary at your old job, or perhaps even a decade's worth of salary, all because of the strong relationship you build over time.

Where do you find the good brokers? One source is www.CCIM. com. That stands for *Certified Commercial Investment Member*, and it's a designation held by only six percent of commercial real estate practitioners. Brokers work hard at a series of courses to earn the CCIM designation. It's a pretty rigorous program and is prestigious in commercial real estate circles. The CCIM website lists CCIMs in each market.

At the same time that you are checking out the source above, go to the commercial property websites at www.loopnet.com and www .propertyline.com. There, not only can you view a variety of current deals, but you can also get a sense of which brokers are active in a market.

Remember in an earlier chapter I recommend that you train brokers who send you bad deals by calling them, thanking them, and explaining what you're looking for. You can use the same approach here. Just call a broker who listed a deal on the Internet and say "I buy properties based on the following criteria. . . . Do you have any other deals that meet these criteria, either on the market now or coming on the market soon?"

You'll strike out a lot, but it only takes one good commercial deal to make your entire year. Plus, the Internet is where the active brokers post their listings. When you see brokers' ads in the Yellow Pages, you don't know when they did their last deal or how active they are. Internet brokers have proven that they are still in the game.

The deals you see on the Internet have been largely picked-over. Still, I've been successful buying properties off the Internet from two sources.

The first is residential brokers. Many of them have not built a list of commercial buyers, so they immediately put properties on the Internet to see if they can sell them quickly and easily. They tend to price the properties so they make sense.

The other source is property owners. Some owners are attracted by the lack of middlemen and fees. I've done a couple of really good deals directly with owners who are just looking to move their properties quickly.

Attorneys

You will need two types of attorneys in a market: The *title attorney* or *closing attorney* will review the deal paperwork, and will create your buying entity to protect your rights. The other attorney will handle any litigation.

The title or closing attorney will be easy to find. Every market has good ones. Get a referral from your local savings and loan, mortgage broker, or property manager.

Always use a local closing attorney when doing business in another state. Consider this: Our 50 states can't even agree on being called *states*. For instance, Massachusetts is a *Commonwealth* and—believe it or not—the official name for Rhode Island is *State of Rhode Island and Providence Plantations*. With that kind of independent thinking, is it any wonder that the states have very different real estate laws?

Make sure you have someone in your corner who knows the state and local laws cold. That person will review your purchase and sale agreement, lender's term sheet, title, survey, and all other closing documents. She will even review the service contracts in place at the property.

She will also negotiate better terms for you, and find loopholes and problems in documents. Avoiding just one of these is worth more than the cost of the attorney. These types of attorneys are usually very nice to do business with.

Your litigation attorney is a different story. Here you want the baddest S.O.B. in the land. You want the guy they tell stories about. That's the same guy that no one wants to be up against in a court case.

Everyone knows who this person is. When you start asking around, one name will pop up over and over.

In my early days I used to sit in the back at housing court and watch the proceedings. I got a free and fascinating education that way, observing the arguments of landlords and tenants. (You should do the same if you intend to buy multi-family properties.)

One attorney stood out from the rest. He was like a legal acrobat: His maneuvers were all legal, but they drove the other side crazy. He was also a junkyard dog, defending his clients' interests at all costs.

A couple of years later, I had to sue a party because it did not do what it promised to do. The first person I called was that attorney. I remember my sister, Tammy, saying, "But Dave, you said that guy was an S.O.B.!" I smiled: "That's right and now the S.O.B works for me!"

I've been in situations where I simply mentioned my attorney's name and the other party backed down. That's a good feeling—and it didn't even cost me a dime in those cases merely to mention his name.

Speaking of expense, you do not need to retain the litigator full time, of course. You only use this person when the need arises, and then it will be expensive. Generally it's worth every penny to have the best people on your side in these situations.

Other Deal Team Members

You'll work with an insurance agent and title agent in the course of doing a deal. Cultivate strong relationships with them, too. They are often well-connected in town, and see high volumes of deals.

They are privy to lots of talk, and sometimes that talk relates to a deal that may soon be coming on the market. For instance, a property owner may casually mention that she will be slowing down, or looking to sell some properties. Your goal is to have these agents thinking of you first when they hear such things.

Be sure to let your network know that you are always looking for new deals. Do not assume that they know this!

YOUR MONEY TEAM

We've already talked at length about how to get the money to fund your deals. Here are a few additional thoughts.

The Mortgage Broker, of Course

As you know, brokers are absolutely crucial to your commercial real estate success. But did you know that they are also free?

A *cost* is something you pay that you don't get back, like gasoline. An investment is something you pay that should come back to you in the form of a return. When you pay a substantial fee to a mortgage broker, you definitely receive a return. That benefit can take many forms:

- Your broker may give you advice that keeps you out of bad deals.
- She may work with lenders to assemble a creative financing package when conventional lenders simply said "no."
- She'll handle issues that arise with the lender—issues that otherwise might stall the deal.
- She might point you in the direction of other excellent team members, such as property managers and property inspectors.

All these services can easily be worth more than the one-point fee you'll probably pay the broker.

It gets better: Because that fee is financed out of the deal, you never reach into your pocket to pay it. In a sense that's better than free: You don't personally pay it, and you get a whole range of professional services. It doesn't get better than that.

Private Money Partners

These team members will give you that last 20 to 30 percent of the funding that you need to get the deal done.

The watchwords for handling these people are *exceed expectations*. That means:

- Under-promise and over-deliver on investment returns.
- Return phone calls and e-mails very promptly. This is not the place for delegation. Working with your money partners is definitely a *highest and best use* of your time.

- Send them detailed monthly reports. They should get a profit-and-loss statement, a budget comparison, a variance report, and an executive summary.

Insider Tip

It's nice to deliver good news, but it's absolutely crucial that you deliver bad news to your money partners. The worst thing you can do is hide bad news, allow it to fester, and then have it come out into the open anyway. Should that happen, your trustworthiness will go down the toilet, along with your reputation. People can handle bad news if they understand why it happened and what you're doing about it.

For example, I was recently informed by the manager of my Arkansas properties that a big hail storm blew through and did a lot of damage to some of our assets. I immediately sent out an e-mail to investors. It explained what had happened and what our plans were to make repairs and to be reimbursed by the insurance companies.

Even if there is no major news to deliver, conduct a conference call each quarter. It's a great way to connect with your money partners, have them hear the answers to everyone's questions, and get briefed on plans for the next period.

One other insider tip: *Never* subsidize the cash flow that you pay out to investors. If your property has the inevitable ups and downs in cash flow, it's a temptation to *smooth them out* by paying out less than you earn in one period and more than you earn in another.

I'm not talking about cash reserves here—of course you should fund your reserve account before paying distributions to investors. What I'm referring to is the artificial manipulation of cash distributions to make them appear more like a bond return.

Investors who are only happy with predictable bond-like distributions should stick to bonds. When you artificially act like a bond, you open yourself up to several possibilities, all of them bad:

- You'll get the wrong type of investors in the deal—ones that cannot handle any risk or variable returns.

- You run the risk of depleting your reserves in order to pay distributions. That has the effect of making things look great—right up to the point that you've exhausted your reserves and are suddenly in deep trouble.
- It masks underperformance of the deal, and thus delays the delivery of that bad news to investors. When you delay bad news, you give an opening to a litigation attorney for investors to claim that you deceived the investors.

Let distributions mirror the actual performance of the property. You will thank me later.

YOUR PROPERTY TEAM

The *deal team* handles the potential investment as it is described on paper, by reviewing financials, market information, and so on.

In contrast, the *property team* is more hands-on with the actual property. You will not only use them after you own the property, but will rely heavily on them during the due diligence period.

Property Manager

Let's say you put a property under contract in an emerging market that is 200 miles away. The numbers seem to work and pictures of the property look good. Your next step is to call the management company that you plan on using and ask them to *shop the property*.

I want them to go over to that property, pretending to be a potential new lease applicant. They will walk through the property and mentally note everything that I should be concerned about.

After all, those nice pictures might have been taken five years ago. They may also have conveniently avoided showing a roof in need of major repair. I will negotiate such big issues before I spend time and money on a property inspection and a trip to see it myself.

A mistake that I see many investors make is to get so excited about putting a deal under contract that they skip the step of having the property shopped. They eventually do find out about the problems, but by then they've invested more time and money. There's a greater temptation to ignore or rationalize the problems at that point.

Your management company will be happy to provide this service, because they look forward to being manager of the property as soon as you close the deal.

The management company will also help to get the deal closed. They'll report to you on a weekly basis about occupancy, collections, work orders, local issues—all the things you need to know in order to negotiate successfully.

After you close on a property, you'll need to manage the management company. That means making sure you continue to get accurate reports regularly. If reporting becomes spotty, it is the first sign that their eye is not on the ball. It's time to sit them down and tell them to get back on track.

Closely watch your collections, occupancy, and expenses. If the management company starts to get lazy or does not perform up to your expectations, you will see poor results in these areas first. Give them one warning to meet minimum standards. If they don't meet your specific performance goals for the next period, fire them.

Contractors

The property manager may have identified a problem while she shopped the property. After you raise that problem with the seller, you may very well have a contractor visit the property to determine the likely cost to fix the problem.

The best way to find contractors in the local market is from referrals from brokers, property managers, attorneys, and all of your other team members.

A good contractor is like gold. Do not become a *doormat*, but do keep them happy. The best way to do this is always to pay them on time, as I mentioned earlier. Don't pay them before the job is complete, but write out that check the instant the job is done. You can be sure the contractor is already chasing many other people for money. When you pay immediately, you will just as immediately become one of his favorite customers. He'll even put off other jobs so he can get your job done.

Property Inspector

Commercial property inspectors cover large territories. Though most areas have one or two good inspectors, it may be necessary to fly your favorite inspector to different parts of the country to go through your properties.

Their job is to review the entire property very methodically and tell you if there is anything wrong. When they find issues, you want estimates of the cost to fix them, even though you will also ask your contractor for estimates.

The inspector will also indicate if the property meets the Americans with Disabilities Act and if the property is properly zoned.

You will receive a comprehensive inspection report. It will not only form the basis of any negotiations on major issues, but will help form the basis for budgeting expenses for several years to come.

Maintenance Specialist

Soon after I began to buy commercial properties, I found that one of the biggest items to deviate from budget was repairs and maintenance. The reason it was so high is because management companies like to subcontract many repairs. They may have a relationship with the contracting company—a relationship that benefits both of them, but not you.

We require that all regular maintenance be done in-house. Sometimes that means the management company must hire another maintenance person to keep up with repairs. I'm okay with that, because the new maintenance salary should cost less than what would be paid to subcontractors.

Your maintenance specialist should be *HVAC certified*. This will save you a lot of money on subcontracting. It would be good if he held electrical certifications as well. A good maintenance staff will not only save you money, but will keep your tenants happy. They'll get repairs done quickly, which will help to justify above-market rents. In turn, that will enable you eventually to sell the property for top dollar.

Now do you see why you'll have no time to lick envelopes and answer the phone? You must get people to do those tasks, so that you can focus on crafting your team in each market.

Some investors make the mistake of putting only a couple of team members in place before they move on to another market. That's no way to extract maximum dollars from one of your target markets. Finish what you start. Get that team fully developed, and you can harvest profits from that market for years to come.

In the Next Chapter

It has been said that you make your profit when you buy a property. That may be true, but it ignores a very important source of additional profit—the way your property is managed while you own it.

In the next chapter we explore in more detail the steps you take to work with the property manager to maximize your current and ultimate paydays.

11

USE A TIME MULTIPLIER

Some things don't change when you become rich. Time, for instance. When you're a working stiff, trying to break out of the 9-to-5 existence, it's easy to lament: "I just don't have time to do anything but work and sleep and work again."

When you're rich, your time is really no different. It's true that you can afford many assistants and specialists, but you may still lament, "If I only had more time, I could do *so-o-o* many more deals."

Earlier we discussed your *money multipliers*—all the financing sources available to you, so that you can get more deals done. We've also covered the key members of your team.

Of all those key members, one specialist has the potential to advance your real estate career more than any other: It's your property manager.

I don't want to get too galactic on you here, but think about it: An effective property manager allows you to transcend both time and space. Not only does that company do the day-to-day work to keep your property running smoothly, but it can happen 2,000 miles away from you.

These companies are true time and wealth multipliers, and deserve a whole chapter of their own.

Amateur Mistake: "I have to see it with my own eyes to know what's going on."

Pilots go through the same phase of believing that they must see it with their own eyes: They grip the cockpit controls and study the scene through the window with all their might. Then, when they decide to become *instrument rated,* they go through the difficult process of learning instead to trust those instruments with their lives. For their examination, they must wear a hood that blocks the view out the cockpit window, allowing them to see only the instruments.

When Air Force pilots are being trained, they'll sometimes hear the actual cockpit audio recording of a pilot who insisted that he was climbing, despite the fact that his instruments said he was level, and so did the control tower. He overcorrected downward, and the recording ends when his plane flies into the ground.

Fortunately, you do not have to trust a property manager with your life, but you should trust him with your investments. You'll have a comprehensive set of instruments—your reports—to tell you exactly how that property is functioning.

Your alternative is to plod along in your comfy, local market, working much harder than you need to, for a much smaller, more local reward.

The Roles of the Property Manager

I have great respect for property managers. After all, when I first invested I tried to *save money* by doing my own management, until I became exhausted, burned-out, and smarter. I turned the management reins over to professionals who do nothing but manage properties, and I became rested, alert, and richer.

Let's look at the main activities that you will monitor as your manager performs them:

Collect and deposit rents. It doesn't get more fundamental than this. Through your real-time access to the property bank account, you'll have independent validation of how much revenue is coming in, and when.

Fill your property with good tenants. Your manager must give you a written marketing plan that shows what they plan on doing to get traffic into your property. They should have proven *closers* on site who have the ability to convert applications into leases. Also notice that I say "good tenants." Any idiot can fill a property by low-balling rents and banging up a sign that reads *Free Beer*. I trust that this is not your target market.

Keep your property full. Tenant turnover will be your biggest expense. Your manager must keep good tenants as long as possible by treating them like the gold they are. This will happen when the property is well-maintained, rents are a good value for the amenities, and tenants are treated with courtesy and respect. Your manager should give you a detailed tenant retention plan that identifies monthly activities focused on keeping tenants happy and in the property.

Effectively handle tenant problems. A tenant may violate a clause in the lease, or not pay all the rent on time. Your manager should work from a set of written policies on how all these circumstances will be handled. Many of them can be handled without any involvement on your part. Sometimes the manager should escalate the issue and at least make you aware of it. If the police are called to a property repeatedly, you want to know that—after the management company has handled the immediate situation.

Oversee repairs and maintenance. Your manager must ensure that tenant work orders are being done in a timely manner. As you now know, lack of response on tenant work orders is the number one reason that good tenants leave. A maintenance log will show what repairs were done when.

Even on the first day that you own the property, you will have a pretty good idea of the correct pace of repairs and improvements to the property, based on your budget and marketing plan.

The log should match that level of activity. If there is less activity, you may be seeing deferred maintenance happening. If there is more activity, then a discussion with the manager is in order to discuss why.

Handle day-to-day operations. This includes the supervision of all employees. If they don't perform up to their agreed-upon goals, then employees must be trained, counseled, and possibly fired, depending on the situation. That's the job of your management company.

Monitor utilities. The management company is the contact for the cable, telephone, gas, and other utility companies. That list will vary, depending on whether *net leases* are in place for tenants to pay utilities. I know it sounds basic, but some managers neglect to pay utility bills in a timely manner. That's why the next item is important . . .

Manage accounts payable. These are the bills that are due but not yet paid on a property. You must see a regular accounts payable report, with logs of these payments happening like clockwork. They will also show up in your profit-and-loss statement. If a property is underperforming, one of the ways that a management company will hide this is by not reporting accounts payable.

Management companies can sometimes be more expert at hiding numbers than at managing the property. I once had a company that did not report accounts payable from vendors that had not submitted a W-9 tax form. It was their *policy*. How convenient, given that it was the management company that had to send out the W-9s to be filled in.

My *policy* was to fire these people, after I discovered this deception, and the tens of thousands of dollars' worth of unpaid bills that I had not known existed.

Prepare other property reports. The management company will be responsible for sending you the same reports that you will send to your investors. That includes a profit-and-loss statement, executive summary, and variance report, which will show any deviations from budget.

Assembling Your Local Property Management Team

The first place to go to find qualified managers is the broker who sold you the deal. He most likely has been in the market for a long time and is painfully aware of who is a good manager and who is not.

The broker's motivation is also aligned with yours: If your property is well-managed, you just might sell the deal down the road through that broker. If he recommends a manager who turns out to be no good, the broker knows that he'll be in the doghouse with you.

You can also get referrals to good managers by going to www. boma.org. This is the *Building Owners and Managers Association*. As the name implies, it's for both owners and managers of commercial property, and it's highly respected. Becoming a member of this organization allows you to network with other building owners, and ask around about good property managers.

Look at the Fit between Property and Manager

If you want to maximize profits and minimize headaches, it's not good enough to get any old commercial property manager. You must get a manager who specializes in the type of property you have.

By *type of property*, I mean that you must look at two different dimensions—*use* and *class*.

Within the *use* distinction, you have retail, office, multi-family, hospitality, warehouse, and so on. Within the *class* distinction, properties are graded from *Class A* to *Class D*.

Class A properties are the newest and have the most credit-worthy tenants. They have higher rents, higher expectations by tenants, and are usually the easiest to maintain. *Class D* properties are on the opposite end of the scale in every respect.

It's a mistake to own a *Class C* property and hire a *Class A* manager. The manager's standards are too high and they will over-improve the property compared to the income potential. Of course, you don't want to do the opposite and get a *bargain-basement Class D* manager for your *Class B* property.

Similarly, it's a mistake to go with a manager whose main experience is multi-family when you have a strip mall to manage, despite their insistence that they are *commercial property managers*.

Ask the prospective management company what type of property makes up the largest percentage of properties that it manages. If this is not the type of property you are buying, move on.

Speaking of property type, one of the highest designations managers can get is *Certified Property Manager*, or *CPM*. It is a distinction granted by the Institute of Real Estate Management and can be researched at www.irem.org.

CPMs are trained in property management for all property types. However, graduates tend to specialize in a particular property type. The nice thing about the IREM web site is that you can plug in which city and property type you are looking for, and the site will return results that match those criteria. If your city does not have any results, then broaden your search to surrounding areas. Managers often work in territories that are larger than the city they're based in.

Most of the larger companies know where their skills lie and will not attempt to take on a property that they do not feel they can be successful at managing. You have to watch out for the smaller management companies, though. They may be looking to increase their business despite their lack of experience in your property type. This is called *going to school* on you. Let some other property owner pay the price to give these companies an education.

I like hiring property management companies that manage lots of units. Some investors think they may get lost in a large company and won't get the individual attention their property needs to be successful.

My experience is that large companies usually have the knowledge and systems in place to ensure that all of their properties are looked after efficiently. The good ones have solid management and monitoring.

The other benefit of going with larger companies is that you can *piggyback* on their insurance, and be insured under their *umbrella* insurance policy. Because they have so many units under management, their insurance premium will be among the lowest. You benefit from their economies of scale for this substantial operating expense.

Insider Tip

When doing your analysis of a property, always use a higher rate for the insurance premium, and don't assume you'll be under someone else's umbrella policy. If for some reason you stop using that management company and go with a smaller firm, your rates will increase. In other words, make sure your deal numbers work at the higher rates.

How to Interview a Management Company

Let's assume that you've used your network to ask about good property managers, and you've narrowed the list to three candidates. They all seem qualified to manage your property, but you want the one that will be the best fit. Here are the questions you should ask each firm.

"What types of properties do you specialize in and what do you feel your strengths are?"

Don't lead them in the question; just ask it and wait.

"How many [units or square feet] of my type of property do you currently manage?"

Of course, if it's multi-family, it will be measured in units, and if it's retail or office space, you'll refer to square feet.

"How many [units or square feet] do you own of my type of property?"

Oddly enough, it may be a red flag if they own too much. You might be hiring your competition to manage your property.

"What are all of the addresses that you currently manage?"

Don't let them *cherry-pick* only a few good addresses for you. Take a ride by ones that you randomly pick from the list when you're in the area. It will give you an idea of how they manage their properties.

Be aware that if you go by a property and the outside looks ratty, it could be due to a number of different causes. Perhaps the manager is doing a poor job, or maybe the owner is not releasing money to have it managed well. If it is the latter, good management companies eventually fire owners who do not give them an opportunity to manage the property correctly.

"What special training do you provide for your managers?"

Continued education is an essential part of a good management company.

"Will you provide written management plans?"

They should provide documents in the form of a marketing plan, company resume, and operational projections, or pro formas, so that you can send these to the bank with your loan package.

"What will be your fee?"

This is an area where you don't want to skimp. Find out what the going management fee is for properties like yours in that area and pay it. You shouldn't pay much more than the average amount, but you don't want to pay less, either. They will only do what they're getting paid for. If they feel underpaid, they will not perform the way you expect.

Management fees are generally a percentage of collected revenues. Do not sign up for a minimum fee. Some management companies try to pull this and it is not in your best interest. In effect, it doesn't matter how much rent they collect, because you'll be willing to pay them a minimum amount. Forget that.

"What is included in that fee?"

Get an itemized list of what is included. For instance, are any salaries included, or advertising? Sometimes nothing is included, and the fee is for their experience in the market. That could be acceptable, depending on what the other management companies are like.

"What will you charge for signing new tenants?"

This depends on the size and type of your project. For office and retail, it could be a fee that's based on a percentage of the lease.

If it is a multi-family property, then it may be one month's rent. If you have a large complex that merits having a leasing agent on site, that person may get a salary plus leasing bonus.

"What is the cost of the eviction process?"

In some states you are required to be represented by an attorney. Other states allow you to use an agent, a role that the property management company can fill. Also ask about the eviction procedure in that state.

Office and retail tenants are usually very easy to evict if they don't adhere to the terms of the lease or don't pay. With multi-family tenants it can get tricky. Depending on how tenant-friendly the state is, evictions can take from three weeks (Texas) to more than three months (Massachusetts).

"What type of advertising do you do, and who pays for it?"

They should be able to answer this question very quickly. They should be active with many forms of advertising, and not just the classifieds, which are the most expensive media to use. You're looking for a response that includes websites, flyers, newsletters, trade magazines, and so on.

Often these are *pass-through* expenses, meaning you will have to pay. Occasionally you can benefit from a general ad that the company runs for many properties, in which case you might pick up only a fraction of the cost.

"What should I expect for monthly reports?"

Even though we know you should be getting several reports at a minimum, it's useful to see what the company thinks is standard procedure. You should expect an executive summary, a profit-and-loss statement, and a budget variance report, at the very least.

"Do you have your own maintenance staff or do you subcontract?"

Watch out for this one. If they subcontract, you'll likely pay much more for repairs and maintenance than if they have their own staff.

On the other hand, if they have their own staff, you must make sure they are not in the maintenance *business*. Sometimes property management companies make more from their maintenance department than from their management fees! This happens because they either overbill you for repairs, or they do more repairs than necessary. They might even bill you for repairs that were never done.

You will only discover some of these practices by asking your network or by experiencing them yourself. When you do hire a company, make sure they know that you are watching maintenance closely. They should stay within the operating budget, adhering to normal standards of maintenance and repair for your type of property.

"What property management software do you use?"

Many good property software packages exist to automate management activities. You should ask whether their system allows you to see your property numbers real-time. You won't have *editing* access to these numbers, but all you need is *viewing* access.

"How do you screen tenants?"

This is a very important question. When you lease to businesses, the tenants are only as good as their credit history, given that leases range from 3 to 20 years. The manager should be scrutinizing each tenant's credit history and business model. Is that business a good fit for your location? Will the business provide a quality, in-demand service for that market?

With multi-family properties, both credit score and income are important. Each property class has different criteria that tenants must meet to be approved. An A property will require substantially higher credit scores and income to qualify compared with a C property.

"Can you give me three references?"

Always ask for references and actually call them. You'll be amazed at how many people give you references that are not entirely positive.

"Will you allow me to be a signor on the operating account?"

You might word it as a request, but it's really a demand. You *must* be a signor on the operating account. That will give you the ability to get to your funds whenever you feel the need.

If your management company is not performing and you find the need to replace them, you don't want your operating account held hostage. They can't legally do this, of course, but they definitely can slow things down, claim that they never received a letter, throw up some legal technicality, and employ other techniques to make your life miserable. In the meantime, your property will need money to cover operations. That money must now come out of your pocket.

Instead, you must have the ability to remove the funds quickly and open a new account to which the management company will not have access.

Here is the objection you may hear from the management company: "We don't allow such access because we've had owners take all the money out of the account at the time of resale. We then were left with final utility bills and vendor bills that were not paid."

You can solve this dilemma in one of two ways: If you really want to work with this company for some reason, offer to open a reserve account and deposit an amount they'll be satisfied with to cover short-falls at closing. The other option is what I usually recommend: Scratch that company off your list of finalists.

"Do you require that I list the property with you at resale?"

Some management companies will put in their contract that you must give them the listing for the property they manage for you when it's time to sell. Otherwise, they require that you pay them a commission at the time of resale, even if you sell it through another broker. In other words, you will pay a double commission.

At the very least, take this absurd requirement out of the contract. Better yet, dump the company: After all, they are a management company, not a brokerage outfit. It's okay to let your manager know that at the time of resale, you will make a decision. If things have worked out extremely well, they'll naturally be a serious contender for the listing. They first must perform.

THE PROPERTY MANAGEMENT AGREEMENT

When you find the best management company for your property, make sure that the agreement protects you and motivates them.

Property management agreements come in many shapes and sizes. Each company will have its own flavor. You can get a pretty good version from either the Institute of Real Estate Management at irem.org or the Building Owners and Managers Association at boma.org. Keep in mind that these outfits will supply contracts that tend to be weighted somewhat toward the property management company, but they're a good place to start.

In any contract there's plenty of *boilerplate*, or language that is common to all such contracts. Let's look at the other, more important items that should and should not be in there.

Spending authority. This clause governs how many dollars a manager can spend before he has to get approval from you. It typically ranges from $500 to $5,000, depending on your comfort level and the property size. If you make it too small, things will not get done because the management company will be constantly waiting for approvals. If the amount is too high, the manager may potentially overspend your money.

Establish what the going rate is by talking with your network of experts in that market, and monitor these expenses. That way, if you set the amount too high or low, you can soon adjust it.

Reserve account. The company may require that you have a certain amount of money in a reserve account at all times to fund operations. If this account is not replenished and the property is under a constant cash crunch, this may be a reason for the manager to terminate the agreement.

Responsibilities. These will be spelled out in the agreement, and will relate to both parties. Your main obligations will be to provide direction, specifications, and plans to the property manager, and to reimburse them for expenses incurred. It is also your obligation to keep the property fully insured. The management company may require that they be put on the insurance policy, so that they will be notified of any lapses.

The management company is responsible for many functions, including marketing, leasing, reporting, maintenance, and so on. They must also abide by equal housing laws and other regulations, and keep the owner's information private.

Performance. If the manager does not perform to certain standards, it can be grounds for termination. For instance, they are required to keep the property leased up to a certain occupancy level.

Accounting. The manager must perform accurate and timely reporting and keep the books in proper order.

Rent. The company must collect and deposit rents daily. Do not let rents hang around the office. The manager also must perform all necessary actions to collect rents and perform evictions if necessary.

Term. The management company will want you to agree to a one-year term. That's okay, as long as there is also a clause that allows either party to terminate the agreement for any reason with a 30-day written notice. This will protect you from poor performance or from a management company that is simply not the right fit for you. It is also an incentive for that company to continue to perform.

Key Information That You Need and How Often You Need It

Definitely get agreement up front about the exact nature of the reports you expect from the management company, in terms of both content and frequency.

What you really need is a *dashboard* that gives you all the information necessary to navigate to your profit destination. I call it the *Monday Morning Report*, because that's when you will see it every week. It can be just one page for each property and it includes:

- Property name.
- Total number of units or square feet.
- Number of units or square feet not currently producing rent, for whatever reason. This may be space that is used for storage, leasing office, and so on.
- Number of units or square feet available for rent.
- Total number of units or square feet occupied last week, converted to a percentage.
- Move-ins for the week.
- Move-outs for the week.
- Evictions during the week.
- Total number of currently occupied units. This gives you a quick look to see if your occupancy since last week has gone up, down, or sideways.
- Number of notices 30 days out. These are tenants who have given notice that they will be leaving within the next 30 days.
- Number of notices 30 to 60 days out. The same as above, but further into the future.
- Total number of units or square feet preleased, that is, tenants moving in within the next 30 days.
- Occupancy projection for the next 30 days.
- Occupancy for the next 60 days. This gives you a great opportunity to change any downward trends before they happen. If you know that occupancy will drop 60 days from now, you have 60 days to correct the problem. The dashboard allows you to look into the future and make necessary changes today.
- Number of work orders submitted.
- Number of work orders completed. If the property is getting backed up on work orders, something needs to change. Perhaps

you must hire extra help to get caught up. A growing number here will result in growing vacancies later.

- Total traffic. The total number of potential tenants who contacted the office, inquiring about a rental.
- Total applicants. Number of inquiries that were converted into applications.
- Total number approved: tenants who were screened, with results that were favorable, and were offered a lease.
- Gross potential rent. Amount the property could collect at 100 percent occupancy.
- Billed rent. Amount actually billed for the month.
- Collected. Month-to-date collections.
- Delinquent. Total amount of rent outstanding.

With this dashboard you can see the health of your property at a glance. Look for trends each week. Take early action to keep your cash flow healthy and your property appreciating. If your manager does not agree to weekly reporting, or does not deliver it, get another company. It means that they are disorganized and will not be able to anticipate trouble before it arises.

You should get other reports on a monthly basis, such as rent roll. It will list the tenants, what they are paying, how much rent is billable, and which tenants are more than 30 days behind.

Also get a copy of the check register showing who was paid what during the month. Review an accounts payable report so that you know who is owed what for work that was completed during the month. Insist on this monthly report and constantly ask the management company if the report is up-to-date and accurate.

In fact, make these accuracy requests in writing. Why? Because management companies sometimes underreport accounts payable. When the time comes for a sale or change in management companies, the owner can be shocked to discover the true—and much higher—amount of accounts payable. It's more difficult for weasels to explain away a trail of written statements that they made.

Next, get two versions of the profit-and-loss statement. One should compare the current month's actual numbers with the operating budget.

The other version is the twelve-month trailing report. It shows you the last twelve months of operating numbers side-by-side, so that you can pick up on trends.

The variance report will explain any items on the profit-and-loss report that came in more than ten percent above or below projections.

Review a copy of the balance sheet, so that you can keep an eye on current assets and liabilities.

Also ask for a list of capital improvements that are either in process or scheduled to be done.

All these reports should be accompanied by an executive summary that succinctly explains highlights from the underlying reports. Categories covered will be revenues, expenses, cash flow, capital improvements, operations, staffing, and miscellaneous.

The executive summary is important because you shouldn't have to go digging for the good or bad news. However, don't simply rely on the summary, but study the numbers yourself.

GIVING UP CONTROL IN ORDER TO HAVE CONTROL

The most successful commercial real estate investors have met the challenge of giving up hands-on, direct involvement with properties. It's painful to do so at first, because our senses of sight, sound, and touch are so strong. It is indeed a challenge to disregard the thought that *I must see and touch my property to know what's really going on* and rely instead on a comprehensive instrument panel.

Someone is definitely hands-on with your property, and it should be your manager, not you. This frees you to go out and do more deals.

Here are several other recommendations that will lift you out of *property management* and into *asset management*, where the big money is.

- **Commit time to the project.** Even though you're not spending your time handling day-to-day responsibilities, you still must commit to investing time and, if necessary, money to the property to ensure that all goes well. Regarding the money commitment . . .
- **Fund reserves with your cash flow before you pay yourself.** Maintain an adequate reserve so that when unexpected capital improvements or repairs occur—and they will—you will have the money to cover them promptly. If you know a big expense will inevitably arise, such as a roof replacement, build up those reserves to prepare for that day.
- **Know your exit strategy when you purchase the property.** Is this a *fix-and-flip*, a long-term hold, or a repositioning to its highest and best use? On day one of your ownership you should already be working steadily toward that goal.

  Of course, this does not mean you are tied to that one exit strategy. New challenges and opportunities will present themselves. That's a reason to reevaluate your existing plan, but not to avoid having one in the first place.
- **Know the market where you buy.** That means knowing your tenant profile, your competition, the current supply-and-demand situation, and also trends into the future. It's a lot of work initially, but just think how much easier it will be to buy your second property in that market!
- **Visit your property every three to six months.** It may be more frequent at first, but when your monitoring systems begin to hum, those visits will become further apart.

  I like to arrive unannounced. That way I can catch people in their regular routines, and see the property as it is normally run. Planned inspections can contain a lot of theater, with a sudden flurry of activity to impress the boss—you.

  Imagine the confidence you'll gain when you make a surprise visit and things are neat, attractive, and working well. Also imagine the message you send with your first surprise visit: *Wow, the owner might show up at any time, so we need to be on our toes.*

Naturally, make sure you reward a company that's doing a great job without having to be told again and again to do it.

On the other hand, if you do happen to give the company notice that you're coming to town—and even then the property seems in bad shape—it's time for a serious discussion about why this happened. It may indicate a poorly run management company. Give them a warning and plan a surprise visit in about 30 days. If your property is in the same condition, give them their notice.

Management companies are key to your ability to grow your company and your fortune. Manage them effectively and you will be successful.

In the Next Chapter

We've covered a great deal of ground in the preceding chapters. But in one sense the best is yet to come—selling your property.

As you know, I'm a big fan of large amounts of cash flow streaming in, month after month, while I hold a property. But nothing comes close to the feeling of finishing a deal and being highly rewarded in the form of a big, fat check.

In the next chapter we take that last step and discover how to maximize your payday.

12

THE RIGHT WAY TO SELL
FOR MAXIMUM PROFIT

You know by now that at each stage of investing in commercial real estate, there's a typical way to do it, and then there's the experienced way. Those of us with experience first tried the typical way, and then found a better approach.

It would be a shame to come this far in the ownership of a property, only to blow it in the final phase and not get maximum profit for your deal. Let's explore the key *dos and don'ts* you must follow when you're getting ready to sell.

 AMATEUR MISTAKE: "I WANT TO WRING OUT EVERY DOLLAR OF PROFIT I CAN."

It's the difference between an amateur and a professional. The amateur thinks in single transactions, while the pro thinks in terms of relationships and long-term income streams.

You know my opinion of the investor who wants to *nickel-and-dime* brokers and sellers on the front end. He's quickly regarded as toxic and will never see another deal from the broker. Let's assume for a minute that this investor did get into a deal—probably his last—and is now trying to cash out.

(Continued)

AMATEUR MISTAKE (*CONTINUED*)

That same nickel-and-dime mentality will compel the investor to extract every last dollar out of the property that he can.

Do not maintain too high a price. Notice that I used the verb *maintain* and not *set*. It's perfectly fine to come out of the gate and set a very high price for your property to see if investors will *bite*. Sometimes they do, and it would be a shame to miss that extra profit, just because you didn't ask for it.

It could be that an investor is coming out of a *Section 1031 like-kind exchange*, must purchase a property of a certain size quickly, and has the money to do it. Other investors may be under pressure to get into deals before a fiscal year or quarter ends. Whatever the reason, it's nice to be the beneficiary of such urgency.

If no one expresses interest at the higher price, smart investors pull back to more of a market price. Dumb investors keep their price right up there with their ego—too high.

Most buyers will put down 20 percent on the property and take out an 80 percent commercial loan. Most lenders will not lend on a property with a debt coverage ratio below 1.2 or 1.25. Remember, that ratio is governed by how much income the property generates. Therefore, setting the price too high—while the income remains constant—means that the debt coverage ratio begins to look bad.

If your property comes in below 1.2, you must either lower your price or the seller must put more money down for the loan to work. Unless you're in a really hot market, don't count on the buyer making a larger down payment.

HOW TO KNOW WHEN TO SELL

Your next moneymaking skill is how to recognize when it's time to take your chips off the table and sell that property.

It depends on your original exit strategy for the property and subsequent events. You may have intended to buy it, fix several problems, and flip it for a nice, quick payday.

You might have recognized that the property was low in the market cycle, and you needed to hold it for three to five years in order to capture maximum appreciation.

Then again, you may have wanted to establish a long-term presence in that market and hold the property for many years. You could be the type of investor who enjoys healthy cash flow and refinances from time to time in order to put some of your equity to work elsewhere. You review your portfolio regularly and sell the lower-performing assets, thus creating an ever-stronger portfolio.

Always Be Watching Job Growth and Supply

For everyone except perhaps the fix-and-flip people, it's important to stay on top of job growth in the market.

Job growth is a great leading indicator. Just as canaries would die and thus warn miners when it was time to get out, you must watch the job numbers closely. I'm not talking about job layoffs: Instead, when you notice that *growth* in jobs is leveling off, it's time to look hard at the market and make a selling decision. If you actually see *declines* in jobs, well, you really need to sit up straight.

How do you get these numbers, by the way? Regularly check in with the building department and economic development department. Watch for trends by comparing the numbers with previous reports you received.

I bought a $10 million property in an emerging market in Alabama with a group of other investors. It performed very well for the first year and into the second. The market continued to enjoy strong job growth—it seemed as though there was a new job announcement every other day.

Though the market continued to climb, we began to notice that permits were being pulled for properties of our type within a mile or two of our property. That was another leading indicator that four new properties would come online near us within the next two years.

If ours was a *C property*, this would have been great. It would mean that the value of the entire area would increase and we would be able to charge higher rents. Moreover, we wouldn't have to worry about our *C* tenants moving to the *A* property, because they would not be able to afford it.

The problem? Our property was a *B*. Those other properties would all come online at about the same time, and they'd be actively cutting their rents to poach *B* tenants from properties like ours.

If our tenants could get brand-new space for the same amount we were charging, and they would get better amenities, too—that would be a *no-brainer*. When our occupancy dropped, so would our net operating income and property value—within the next two years.

Our regular check-in with the building department gave us the information we needed to know that now was the time to sell. We could have stuck it out if our plan were to hold properties in that market for the long term. It wasn't. We therefore grabbed the $4 million profit while the *grabbing was good*.

Leave Some Meat on the Bone

This is solid advice, regardless of your exit strategy.

If you're a fix-and-flip investor, you'll do your flip that much faster if your deal is attractively priced.

If you're selling after there's been a big run-up in prices, this is definitely the time to leave some profit in the deal for the next buyer. You do that by selling into strength, and by definitely not waiting until you see the market flattening before you sell.

Look, your buyers are watching that market, too. If they see nothing but strength at the time you are selling, the transaction will be a breeze. If both you and they are watching the gathering clouds, you will really have to discount your deal to make it move.

Here's an easy way to look at it: Sell when your friends and family say you're crazy.

"Dave, the market's so strong!"

"Dave, we've had nothing but good news for several years now—how could you possibly think about selling?"

"Dave, if you wait another six months, you can probably add a fast million to your profit."

What they don't understand is that I'm dying to yank my money out of this strong market, and put it into another market that's been weak for so long. They will tell me I'm crazy again—this time for investing in the midst of weakness.

Don't look back. Do not second-guess yourself by thinking "If only I had known to wait until April, I could have hit the very top of the market."

I will go so far as to say that you should kick yourself if you ever do sell at the peak of a market. It will mean that you were not watching the fundamentals of that market, and that you recklessly waited so long that you risked selling at a bad price. If any *hiccup* happened with the buyer's financing, or with some environmental review, you really would have been up a creek.

Also remember that when a market goes south, it can happen in a hurry. Most investors find comfort in being human sheep. They move in great herds, not really knowing what they're doing but being cozy in the knowledge that all the other sheep also don't know. No one can point a finger only at them.

When the herd catches a whiff of a problem, you better watch out! There's a stampede. Suddenly, all of the sellers who were *waiting for the peak* now panic and dump their properties on the market.

Oh no! They each are now competing with a pile of deals that came out of nowhere! So the price-cutting begins. Now a malaise sets in, fueled by journalists. Articles appear about the negative news: Properties are taking longer to sell, other properties that are still in the construction phase will make the situation worse when they come online, prices are being cut, and so on.

You want to be watching this stuff play out in your rearview mirror, with a sly smile on your face and a mountain of dough in the back seat. Leave the carnage behind.

How to Get Your Property Ready for Sale

It doesn't matter what type of property you have (office, multi-family, retail, warehouse, *A*, *B*, *C*, or *D*): To get maximum dollars for it, you must prepare your property.

Let's first consider how to make it look good physically. Do a complete review of the exterior. Could the landscaping use a facelift, in the form of fresh flowers, trimmed shrubs, and reinvigorated grass? I was a broke landscaper before I became a rich investor. I continue to be amazed by how sellers neglect to spend a few dollars to make their properties look like a million bucks.

Does the signage need freshening? Also review the building exterior, looking for peeling paint, cracks, holes, and so on. Check the mailboxes and parking lot, too. Walk that property with your broker or with someone else who doesn't have a motivation to say "everything's fine." Make a list on the spot, and then get names next to dates to ensure that all the work gets done. You want to be in a position where a potential buyer isn't walking around, mentally deducting property value for each flaw.

Now go into the common areas, such as foyers and hallways. Are they well-lit and do they appear neat and clean? What about the utility rooms and vending areas? Is the boiler room clean? Is the boiler *itself* clean? You should know that when a functioning boiler is dirty, the buyer will conclude that there is something wrong with it. This is true of all mechanical and structural components. Clean them up and put a fresh coat of paint on them if appropriate. Paint probably has the highest return on investment of any improvement you can implement. Make the place look as though it's run with military precision.

Of course, you should also determine what needs fixing and updating in each unit. Not only get that current list of work orders down to zero, but actively look for what will add value at a reasonable cost.

How to Get Your Financials Ready for Sale

The first thing to do when you decide to sell is to create a target net operating income. You must know where you need that NOI to be in order to get the sale price that you want.

Determine this by taking a look at recent sales in the area for properties like yours. If you don't already know, ask your broker network for the current cap rate for properties like yours. Remember, you take the NOI and divide it by the cap rate to determine value.

If properties like yours are trading between an 8 and 9 cap, so will yours. Don't kid yourself. Prepare your property to get the highest dollar for it, but also be realistic. Again, it's okay to go out initially high, but then be prepared to drop that price if there are no takers at the higher-than-market level.

Back to the NOI: Target what you want for a price and then figure out what NOI will get you there. It goes without saying that only two things will get you from where you are now in NOI, to that target number—increased revenues or decreased expenses.

On the revenue side, you can raise rents as leases expire. If you are paying for utilities now, you could institute a bill-back system. Keep in mind that tenants under an existing lease will not be required to pay it. Also, it could harm your competitive position in the market, depending on what other, similar properties are doing.

In my experience, if you send letters to all tenants about billing-back the utilities, about 40 percent will voluntarily start paying. That can be a nice, quick boost to your NOI and property value.

Take a look at your collections. Tighten the system if you are not getting very close to 100 percent collections over the course of the month. What about late fees? If you do not charge for late payments, start.

You should have been on the lookout for these revenue opportunities all along, but better now than never.

Next, focus on decreasing expenses. Begin to judge expenses against your projected sales date. Is it a necessary expense, or can it be put off until after the sale without affecting it?

What about your vendor contracts? Now is a good time to rebid them and see if you can get lower prices. For every dollar you decrease expenses, you add a dollar to cash flow and multiple dollars to your property value.

Take a look at utilities from a different perspective: Have they been trending at the same level or slowly increasing? If it's the latter, find out why. Water leaks are especially common. When you see unexplained patches of greener grass, you may have a cracked pipe. Don't stop looking until you have the answer to the jump in utilities. Even something like repairing leaky faucets and toilets can save as much as 30 percent in monthly water bills. That's huge.

When you do incur expenses, look to see whether you can put them *below the line*. In other words, you may be able to turn them into a *capital expense*.

Operating expenses are good while you own a property, because these regular expenses lower your NOI and your taxable income. On the other hand, capital expenses are depreciated over the life of the property and do not decrease your NOI.

Each time you have an expense, you have a decision: Is it an operating or capital expense? Where you are in the ownership cycle will determine how you answer that question.

If you still have a couple of years or more of ownership, claim as much as you can as operating expenses in order to save on taxes. If you're close to a sale, then claim as much as you can as capital expenditures so that you can keep your NOI higher and thus maintain a higher selling price.

Your accountant will be a crucial team member for these decisions. The IRS has pretty strict rules about how expenses are classified.

The accountant will help you to get the best tax treatment and still have a solid basis for your claims.

Be a *forward thinker*. Just as you should anticipate where the local real estate market will be months and years ahead, you should give yourself time before you put a property on the market.

Your decision to sell should ideally occur at least a year before you actually announce that you're selling. Not only does that give you time to make adjustments and improvements, but those activities will now be reflected in the profit-and-loss statement for all buyers and lenders to see.

The Secret to Preparing a Killer Property-Information Package

Want a real insider tip? Start preparing for the sale *from the very moment you purchase the property*. Set up a system of folders to track your income, expenses, contracted services, repairs, and all other items you reviewed during the due diligence period. You wanted to know that information, and probably had to wait while your seller assembled it. You will now hand the whole thing—all professionally packaged—to your prospective buyer, and blow him away.

Not only is it impressive, but just think of the time it will save you. Instead of spending days trying to reconstruct activities that happened years earlier, you will have it all handy.

Your reputation among brokers will grow even better, and you will get to the closing table that much sooner.

Do You Need a Broker?

My answer is a firm *maybe*.

What with all the commercial-property web sites out there now, it is indeed possible for owners to sell their properties directly. You *will* get callers and *will* save a commission.

Before you conclude that this is the way to go, I have three questions to ask you:

1. **Do you have the time to sell it yourself?** Maybe you do. If so, why aren't you spending that time researching other high-potential markets and building your information networks there?

2. **Are you experienced enough to sell the property yourself?** Do you know what questions to ask a buyer? Do you know what information you'll need from a buyer and what actions you need the buyer to take to ensure that you have a good transaction?

    Inexperienced sellers frequently will take a property off the market to work with a buyer. They get quite far into the process only to see the deal fall apart because that highest-bidding buyer could not get financing.

    When you sell through a good broker, that person has a very large list of buyers he can call to present your deal. He already knows which buyers are *closers*. If you want to sell quickly, the broker will hit those proven buyers and potentially save you a lot of grief.

    If for some reason the broker's top-tier buyers don't bite, the broker will still have a large network to shop your deal to. Your broker will quickly be able to size up any potential buyers for you.

    Want another reason to use a broker? The good ones have been through the closing process countless times before. They know how to overcome obstacles before they become *deal breakers*. The worst-case scenario is that they know when a deal simply cannot go through, so you can get your property back on the market quickly.

    If you bought a property through a broker and you want to do more deals with that person, you really should list the property with her. She will be expecting the listing. If you give it to her, you're now that much higher on her inner circle of contacts. If you don't, you've just dropped way down.

3. **Is saving the commission resulting in a major lost opportunity?** Brokers make their money by buying and selling properties for investors. If you decide to be cheap and *save the commission*, you've just saved a few bucks, but lost a lot more bucks.

You will never see the cash flow and appreciation from the sweet deals that the broker will never show you. She will send them to me instead, because I'm smart enough to take very good care of the brokers who take care of me. The real money is in the relationship, and it can be worth millions of dollars to you over time, if you handle it right.

SELECTING A BROKER

Let's say that something happened to the broker from whom you originally bought the property. Perhaps there never was a broker, because you bought it directly from a seller. Maybe your broker retired or otherwise is no longer on the scene. If you're in this position, the question is how to find the right broker through whom to sell your deal.

Your first choice should be other brokers with whom you've been communicating in that market. Maybe one has been sending you deals while you owned that first property. He's been thinking of you, and now you can return the favor.

When you give them a listing of a property that they didn't originally give you, you will rise pretty high on their *best clients* list. Now you'll see even better deals from them.

If no broker fits that description, your next choice is to seek out a broker with whom you want to do business. When I enter a marketplace, I look for two types of brokers: the *movers and shakers*, who do most of the business in that market, and the *up-and-comers*. A quick way to get the attention of the movers and shakers is to sell your deal through them. This establishes you as an instant *performer*, an instant revenue source.

When you sell your deal through the *up-and-comers*, you're even more quickly recognized as a player, and will instantly become a VIP. They are hungry, and you just provided them with lots of meals. You can expect a nice favor in return, in the form of a sweet deal that they come across.

Perhaps you are selling your one property in a market you have no intention of staying in. In that case, you can also consider offering your deal through one of the big national firms.

These outfits do have major databases of potential buyers and a lot of marketing clout. Then again, the local brokers know most of the local investors.

You'll just have to interview a few and find out what their strengths and weaknesses are. The first objective is to establish what price they think they can get for the property. Compare that with the price you determined earlier, based on your NOI target and known cap rates for deals like yours.

You know what your aggressive price is and also your conservative price. Be wary of the broker who tells you he can get a price above your aggressive price. Some people are just big talkers. They give you inflated prices, get you excited, and then ask for a price reduction after the listing doesn't sell, blaming it on the market.

Find a broker who comes in at the same range you did. He may even say that you could sell for a higher price, but that it will depend on the right buyer coming along at the right time. That's a realistic statement and a good sign.

Conversely, beware of the broker who tries to undercut your deal. He comes in at the lower end of your range and tries to sell you on listing it and pricing at that lower point. This person is looking for a quick commission. He knows he will not have many expenses associated with your listing because it will sell quickly. He's doing you no favors.

If you're in the position of having two or three brokers who pass your test and are finalists, pick the beauty queen based on the best marketing campaign. Make an appointment with each broker and ask him to *sell you your own property*. That's right, ask him to pitch you the property so you can see what he will be telling potential buyers.

The broker should have a multicolored, multipage brochure made up, describing the property, selling the highlights, and laying out the numbers. If a broker can't be bothered to make a brochure because he's not sure if he will get the listing, that broker is not the right one. Look for hungry brokers who are happy to go the extra mile.

Other questions to ask about their marketing campaign are: how big is their list; how big are the lists within the office (not the broker's personal list); what web sites will the property be featured on; and will they advertise in the classifieds. Good marketing campaigns are multi-dimensional, as you know.

How Much Should You Pay in Commission?

That depends on how well you negotiate. In general, the higher the property price, the lower the commission percentage.

Commissions can go as high as eight percent of the purchase price. More common are commissions around six percent. As the price breaks the million-dollar mark, commissions start to trend downward. At $5 million, they drop a little more. The same is true at $10 million and $20 million. Won't it be nice when you're selling your properties for $10 to $20 million! Everything I've been covering in this book is intended to get you there.

I've seen commissions as low as one percent, but that's unusual. Even with deals worth many millions of dollars, commissions usually bottom out at around two percent.

Insider Tip

If a broker sent you a deal that you did and now are looking to re-sell, do not try to negotiate a below-market commission with that person. If you do, she will not send you more deals. Why should she, when she knows that investors like me will be happy to pay them the full-market commission on properties she gave me? Focus on that all-important relationship with the broker.

I just told you not to be cheap. Here's how brokers sometimes get greedy: Some will tell you that you must pay a six-percent commission when a four-percent one is warranted. They'll justify it by saying: "Four percent is too low; nobody in this city will cobroker this deal for a four-percent split."

What the broker just told you is that he doesn't believe he can sell it on his own. He's going to rely on his competition to bring their buyers to the table, too. You do not want this broker.

The Listing Agreement

You've chosen the winning broker and now it's time to sign the listing agreement. It will spell out how long the agreement will be active, what type of *agency* the agreement is, what duties the listing broker will perform, and the amount of the listing commission.

Term

The general term of a listing agreement is 180 days. Some will try to get you to sign for a year. Don't do it. If you do, you've just put yourself into a position of weakness. If the broker doesn't perform, you will be at the mercy of the brokerage agency to release you from the listing so that you can find someone else to sell it for you.

Sometimes you can get a 90-day agreement, but it's rare. If you do get a 90-day one, you can be sure the broker will be very aggressive about selling that property within such a short window.

There is some validity to the argument that 90 days is too short, because the broker will not have enough time to market the property effectively. Brokers hesitate about spending lots of money on marketing only to have the agreement expire when things were getting good. Shorter is not necessarily better.

Types of Agency

The brokerage agreement will cover a concept called *agency*. Agency spells out to whom the broker has a fiduciary responsibility. There are three types of agency: *buyer's*, *seller's*, and *dual*.

With a buyer's agency, the broker has a fiduciary responsibility to the buyer. He works on behalf of the buyer's best interest at all times. That means if the buyer tells the broker something confidential to the deal, the broker will not tell you.

When you're buying properties, some brokers ask you to sign an exclusive buyer's agency agreement. When you sign this, you have agreed that the broker represents you in all transactions in a particular location. Do not sign this agreement. Even if a broker says that he will not work with you unless you sign the agreement, don't sign it. Go to another broker.

Such an agreement would prevent you from working with listing brokers. You need the freedom to be able to work with all brokers in any market at any time.

The most common type of agency that your broker will have you sign is the *seller's agency* agreement. In this arrangement, the broker's fiduciary responsibility is to you alone. Everything the broker knows about you and the property is completely confidential, unless the broker knows that there is a reportable issue with the property, such as hazardous waste. During negotiations, if your broker tells the buyer that he thinks you might accept an offer of a certain amount, he will have violated the agency agreement.

Finally there is the *dual agency* agreement. This happens when a broker has signed a seller's agency with you and is supposed to be working for you alone—but he then brings you a buyer. Now he's in a difficult situation: He needs to work for you alone, but naturally wants to please his buyer, too. In this situation, your broker may come to you and request that the agreement be changed to a dual-agency one. That way he can be fair to both sides.

Some sellers allow this and some don't. In my opinion, it's reasonable to agree to the dual agency, because again, you're in this business for long-term relationships with good, honest brokers.

Performance

The *performance clause* in the listing agreement states that the broker will do everything in his power to bring the seller a *ready, willing, and able buyer*. If for some reason the seller does not feel the agent has performed to this level, the seller may elect to be removed from the agreement.

There will be another clause in the agreement that states that if the seller is introduced to a buyer (from the broker) who buys the property within six months of the expiration of the listing agreement, the seller agrees to pay the broker a commission. This is fair. It protects the broker from a seller asking to be removed from a listing agreement, only to sell the deal to a buyer to whom the broker introduced the seller.

I've seen this happen three times in my own brokerage business. I introduced the buyer to the seller. They then contacted each other directly, and the seller decided to back out of our listing agreement. Their logic was that the seller could avoid paying my company the commission, and the buyer would get a lower price. I would be left with nothing, even though I had introduced them to each other.

Because most states disclose the names of buyers and sellers in each real estate transaction, it's not hard for brokers to notice when, a couple of months later, a property changes hands between the very parties that the broker brought together. In these three cases, I filed a lawsuit against the sellers for the amount of the commission and won.

Commission

The commission is, of course, stated in the listing agreement. The seller agrees to pay that percentage of the sales price if and when a sale is completed during the listing period.

Types of Listings

Just as there are different types of agency, there are three different types of *listings* you can sign with your brokerage company.

1. **Open listing.** This agreement allows the broker and anybody else to sell the property and get a commission. Avoid this listing. It sounds good to have everybody working for you, but in reality you'll have nobody working for you. People will not spend money advertising your property or putting together a decent marketing campaign. After all, their work could easily be wasted if someone else comes out of nowhere and brings a qualified buyer to you.

   The reality of doing an open listing is that the only person working hard on the marketing will be you. If you feel you have the ability to market that property yourself, have at it. Remember my advice, though, about how saving a few bucks on commissions will cost you far more in missed relationship opportunities.

2. **Exclusive agency listing.** This agreement states that the only entity that can sell the property is the brokerage company and it does not have to pay a commission to any cobrokers. Do not sign this one, either, even though brokers will try to get you to agree to it. If you do, you will have just eliminated a very large pool of buyers.

   No other broker or brokerage company other than the company you signed the agreement with will bring you a buyer for your property. Let me be more specific: Others *can* bring you a buyer, but they won't get paid for it; same difference.

3. **Exclusive listing.** This is the type of agreement that you should sign. It states that the brokerage company has the sole right to market and sell the property and will be compensated when a sale is consummated. If there are any cobroker opportunities, those agents also will be compensated. This allows your property to be marketed effectively. It will be seen by the greatest

number of eyeballs, offering you the highest probability of getting the price you're after.

How to Research Your Buyer

You methodically picked the best broker. Now, with offers coming in, it's time to pick the best buyer. The first step is to research that buyer.

The most important question to ask is, "Is he a proven closer?" More specifically: "How many deals of this size has he closed in the past?" This will give you an indication of the buyer's experience and the probability that he will close on your deal, too.

The next key question is to find out where he will get the money for the down payment. It's smart to require *proof of funds*. That means that the seller will show you a letter from his lender, indicating that the down payment funds are in fact available. The last thing you want to have happen is to take your deal off the market, get to the closing, and find that the buyer's financing cannot come together.

Some investors are pretty creative: I know a guy who routinely goes right into closings and tells the seller that he doesn't have enough money to close. He then says the seller has a choice—he can either give him a second mortgage for the balance needed, or he can walk away from the deal.

This is a total psychological ploy on the buyer's side because he knows by the closing that the seller has already spent the money in his mind. He will already have plans to buy a second home, new car, or maybe another property. The seller is psychologically vulnerable at this point, and the buyer knows it.

The majority of the time, the buyer gets the second mortgage! Sure, the seller is not happy, but he'd be even less happy if both the deal and his dreams fall through. Once in a while a seller will tell the buyer what he can do with his *lack of funds*, and the deal's off. That's when the buyer makes a phone call and miraculously comes up with the money.

Beware of investors like this. They have no integrity. And get that *proof of funds* document.

Also ask for a financial history from the buyer. You're unlikely to get a pile of tax returns, but it would be reasonable to get a letter from his lender stating that he is qualified to take down the deal.

Make sure you get a big enough deposit to keep the buyer in the deal. Many buyers naturally want to put down as little as possible, and some will even suggest with a straight face that a few dollars should be sufficient. That's when you simply smile and suggest that a few percent of the purchase price would be sufficient—say, one to three percent. The bigger the deal, the lower the percentage.

If you're smart, you'll get a down payment before the due diligence period and then ask for more money when the buyer signs off on the due diligence. This would mean that all of the buyer's deposits into the deal would be considered *hard*—in other words, if he walks away, he loses it all. It's a good way to keep him in the game. If he doesn't want to put up any additional funds, perhaps he isn't serious after all.

A few buyers will put money down *hard* right at the offer stage. I like these buyers! They let you know they are committed to the deal by giving you tens of thousands of dollars that they know they'll not get back unless they close. That gets my attention.

Why would a buyer do this? He may already have done a lot of the due diligence and likes what he sees. He may know it's a competitive situation, wants the property, and is willing to take a risk to get it. He correctly knows that by going hard early, he's telling the seller he is a closer, and if the seller takes the offer, the deal is very likely to happen.

Google Is Your Friend

It's true that some of the best things in life are free. When it comes to real estate transactions, your use of the free Google search engine is definitely a wonderful thing.

Google your buyer and find out everything you can about him. Sometimes you'll verify that the buyer is indeed credible and substantial. Other times you'll come up with very surprising results.

I was putting together a four-property, mixed-use commercial deal in Louisiana. I got the property package and financials, and formulated my strike price. Shortly before the negotiations, I Googled the seller's name.

I discovered the seller was not a U.S. citizen, and that the properties were in foreclosure. Do you suppose my strike price came down just a little bit, due to the fact that I knew the seller had urgent reasons for selling?

I kept reading and discovered that the seller had three other properties that had been foreclosed on in the past couple of years. I even found a federal court judgment on the Web that stated that if he did not dispose of all his U.S. real estate assets within the next 18 months, the seller was going to jail. Well then.

I later found out what the seller's scam was: He would come into the United States, buy a property, put as little money down on it as possible, and then stop paying everything. I mean everything. He'd collect the rents until someone would buy the property from him.

Some tenants would leave, but others stuck around. Before the bank could actually foreclose some months later, he would declare bankruptcy, after having sent big bags of money to some offshore bank account.

Some business model. All it took was for me to check him out on Google and I had all the information I needed.

For a few dollars you can even go to a service such as www.elance. com and hire professional researchers to do a comprehensive web search on anyone or anything. It's cheap insurance.

It goes without saying that when you are on either side of the transaction, you should use the Internet to get all the information you can on the other party.

FOLLOW UP, FOLLOW UP, FOLLOW UP

You're now very close to selling your deal. Don't blow it by failing to follow up. If you've done your due diligence on the buyer and he checks out, you'll be moving forward with the purchase and sale agreement.

Then the due diligence period will involve lots of questions and *back-and-forth*. The buyer's lender will have its own list of *To Dos*.

Make sure that things don't grind to a halt with each side waiting on the other for something. Check in regularly with your attorney and broker, who in turn should be contacting their counterparts with the buyer.

Stay on top of the dates for the inspection, appraisal, survey, and title work. Know when they were ordered and get dates for when they are due. Don't just wait until something is overdue to start asking questions, but check to make sure they're coming along.

If you don't check up on these items, one or more of them will not get done. Also contact the buyer's bank and make sure they have ordered and received their reports.

Regularly check in with the buyer's attorney, closing attorney, and your own attorney. The buyer's attorney or title company should be completing the title, the purchase and sale agreement, and its review of the closing documents. The lender's attorney should be preparing the closing documents, the note, and the closing statement. Your attorney should be prepared to do whatever is necessary for you to close the loan, including checking the closing statement for accuracy.

Determine whether the buyer has lined up his insurance policy. Simply go back to the checklist that you used when you closed on the property as the buyer, and use that list as a guide for what your buyer must now do.

Could you make the argument that the buyer is a big boy and should be able to do all this stuff without prompting? Yes, you could. That should be a great comfort to you when the deal falls through and you're at some bar, slumped over a drink.

The Closing

If you take my advice and stay on top of the transaction until the very end, you'll find the closing to be a breeze.

You will also have established yourself as the new *rising star* of commercial real estate in that market—and rightly so.

Will you encounter challenges along the way, and maybe a setback or two? Probably. But by following proven systems and always investing with integrity, you will have avoided countless pitfalls that your competition ran right into.

Aristotle Onassis, one of the richest men in the world in the twentieth century, said, "That first $100,000 is the hardest." Trust me when I say that your first deal will be the very hardest.

Think of what you'll have after the first deal: Your team will be in place. You will have established yourself in a market with a reputation as a closer. You'll know in your bones that there's no black magic to getting a deal done, but just a step-by-step, proven path.

You will have received something else: A series of monthly cash flow checks and one big fat one at the end of the deal. You will be chomping at the bit to do a second deal, and soon a third.

Congratulations at taking the most difficult step of all, which is to get motivated to buy and read this book. After all, it's easy to believe that Donald Trump can do deal after deal, but it's a leap of faith to believe that you can start down that road, too.

You are indeed now on that road to wealth through commercial investing. Just be sure that you keep taking steps toward your destination. Do not close the cover of this book without first taking out a piece of paper and writing down the next few actions that you promise to take.

They can be to review certain chapters, then to start getting hooked into your local real estate investing association. Identify a market that looks promising and begin to cultivate relationships with brokers there.

There are only two things that will get you to serious commercial real estate wealth quickly: The first is taking action. Without action, everything is just an empty dream.

The second is increasing your knowledge. If you're really impatient about getting on the *fast track* to becoming a commercial real estate investor, you should consider attending a multiday live event. There you can get every single question answered and concept clarified, when otherwise they may be holding you back from taking action.

You'll also meet like-minded people at all levels of experience, from beginners all the way to seasoned commercial investors. It's astonishing what can happen when you get away from people who hold you back, and surround yourself with people who share a can-do attitude and a desire for financial freedom. You can find more information about current opportunities at www.commercialrealestateinvesting.com.

Welcome to one of the most exclusive clubs of all—the amazing freedom and wealth that comes from being a commercial real estate investor.

Index

SPECIAL BONUS #2

FREE Advanced Training

If you're serious about investing in commercial real estate, you need to know everything you can about what you're doing. Trump University offers its members free continuing education events around the country so that they can stay current on the latest investing trends and strategies. These invitation-only events feature three-days of intensive training where you will learn how to:

- Develop a winning investment strategy
- Build a long-term portfolio
- Finance your deals with minimal capital
- Invest in projects out of state
- Use the internet to source profitable deals

To receive an invitation to the next training event in your area simply register by logging onto:

TrumpUniversity.com/Bonus2

SPECIAL BONUS #3

Wealth Builders Network 14 day FREE Membership

Now that you're a part of the Trump University community we would like to offer you a free trial in the Wealth Builders Network, our premium membership community. As a member you will be able to

- Participate in live training webinars every week
- Access a forms library for invaluable contracts, etc.
- Network with other success-oriented entrepreneurs
- Read the monthly magazine featuring Donald Trump—packed with investing tips and tactics
- View archived webinars
- Download audio classes to your iPod

To accept this free trial invitation please log onto:

TrumpUniversity.com/Bonus3

SPECIAL OFFER FOR READERS OF COMMERCIAL INVESTING 101

If you like what you read in this book, then there's more where that came from.

We understand that the small minority of true "take action" people generally can't get enough information. Therefore we want to make it easy to take the next steps toward your success in commercial real estate.

We've prepared a special bonus for you. All you need to do is go to www.commercialrealestateinvesting101.com and type into the search box the phrase Reader Bonus.

You'll see an impressive collection of tools and resources that we have put together. It includes several back issues of David Lindahl's Real Estate Insights newsletter, special reports on financing your deals, a CD/DVD set, and even a full-color poster that details the entire real estate emerging market cycle.

Again, congratulations for getting and reading this book. We stand ready to provide even more tools and systems to ensure your commercial real estate investing success.